Game Book

ALSO BY MACDONALD HASTINGS

The 'Mr Cork' Books
CORK ON THE WATER
CORK IN BOTTLE
CORK AND THE SERPENT
CORK IN THE DOGHOUSE
CORK ON THE TELLY

Historical Novel
A GLIMPSE OF ARCADIA

Autobiography
PASSED AS CENSORED
JESUIT CHILD
AFTER YOU, ROBINSON CRUSOE

Anthology
MACDONALD HASTINGS' COUNTRY BOOK

Text Books
CHURCHILL ON GAME SHOOTING
HOW TO SHOOT STRAIGHT
SHOOTING: WHY WE MISS
ENGLISH SPORTING GUNS
WHEELER'S FISH COOKERY BOOK (with Carole Walsh)
LONDON OBSERVED (with John Gay)

Biography
THE OTHER MR CHURCHILL
MARY CELESTE
DIANE, A VICTORIAN

For Boys
EAGLE SPECIAL INVESTIGATOR
ADVENTURE CALLING
THE SEARCH FOR THE LITTLE YELLOW MEN
MEN OF GLORY
MORE MEN OF GLORY

For Little Children
SYDNEY SPARROW

For Television
CALL THE GUN EXPERT (A Series)
RIVERBEAT (Two Series)
VOYAGE INTO ENGLAND (A Series)
IN DEEPEST BRITAIN (A Series)
THE HATED SOCIETY: THE JESUITS

Game Book

Sporting Round the World

Macdonald Hastings

LONDON
MICHAEL JOSEPH

First published in Great Britain by Michael Joseph Ltd
52 Bedford Square, London WC1
1979

© 1978, 1979 by Macdonald Hastings

ISBN 0 7181 1768 9

Typeset in Great Britain by
D. P. Media Ltd., Hitchin, Hertfordshire
Printed and bound by Billing & Sons Ltd., Guildford, Surrey

To
my son Max,
who asked me to write this – and for
Charles, my grandson,
in the hope that he will one day read it.

Contents

Contents

Contents

Illustrations

Acknowledgement

Many of these essays were first published in *Gamekeeper and Countryside*. I am grateful to its editor, Mr Edward Askwith, and to Mr John Eadie of Gilbertson and Page for the spur they gave to my pen. Others were originally published in the Country Gentlemen's Association magazine.

At five o'clock this morning the dawn was breaking red
When I put on my shooting boots and shot right out of bed
With pockets full of cartridges I strolled across the lea
While I was after partridges, the Squire was after me
And, heavens, how we shot!
I'll tell you what we got:

CHORUS

Sixteen beaters, a keeper and a cow;
The Postman, the Dustman, the Barmaid at the Plough
What shots! Pot shots!
How the welkin rang!
Oh, what a wonderful time we had!
Bang! Bang! Bang!

An Edwardian Music Hall lyric,
sung by Nellie Wallace.

1

THE MIND OF A CHILD

The outbreak of the Kaiser's War – the impact it made on me in
Pickwick Road, Dulwich – the value of horse manure – my father
joins the army – a successful writer, he takes me to the country – I
am billeted with a farm worker – I make a country friend after my
own heart – my father disapproves of my behaviour – I am ordered
to boarding school – after the war, when I am taken seriously ill, I
find a new life beside the seaside.

I doubt if I would have had the wonderful times I have had
in my life, at any rate they would have been different, if it
had not been for the outbreak of the Kaiser's War. In
August 1914, I was, as the infants' school reports have it
4.10 years old. Through the mind of a child, I remember the
days when 'the lights went out in Europe'. I remember
them precisely.

My parents had a house on the outskirts of London in
Dulwich, which was then a village. The road in which we
lived was called Pickwick Road, because Dulwich was the
place to which Mr Samuel Pickwick reputedly retired after
his adventures. All the houses in the street were named after
places in the chronicles of the Pickwick Club. The house on
the corner was called Dingley Dell. Ours was 'Weller
Willa', which led somebody to ask whether it had an
Australian connection. The road had a peculiar fascination
for me, because in those days of horse-drawn traffic my
father gave me a penny for any pailful of horse manure I
brought in for the garden. In the money values of that time I
was well paid. A penny was worth four liquorice strips
for a farthing each. I waited hopefully when Mudie's cart
delivered my father's books from the lending library, and
the brewer's dray brought the beer (and, with luck, the
brewer's men gave me a handful of bungs which I could use
as soldiers). I always had a lump of sugar to welcome the

17

horse when my father came home in a hansom cab. Sometimes the horse obliged me on our own doorstep. I was another penny in pocket.

A penny, with Britannia leaning trident in hand on the reverse, was also the coin which my father gave me on the day war was declared. Until then, I was unaware that there were other places in the world beyond Pickwick Road and the Dame's school, where I was taken by the nursemaid for lessons. When I heard my parents discussing Belgium, Serbia, France, the explosion points at that time in Europe, the reporter-to-be in me pestered them with questions. My father told me that we were at war with Germany. I asked what that meant and he got rid of me by saying that the Germans would march down Pickwick Road, playing their bands. If we did not throw pennies to them they would kill us. He gave me a penny, and I posted myself at a window on the look out for them.

In retrospect, I feel it was a cruel deception on me, although I cannot recall that I felt any sense of alarm at the time, only a temporary disappointment when the Germans failed to materialise. Within a year I was collecting military brass buttons and soldiers' cap badges, and my mother sewed corporals' stripes on my overcoat.

My father joined the army as a private in the King's Royal Rifle Corps at Winchester, and because he was certified as unfit for active service he was drafted into a labour battalion to dig trenches. However, he was never actually sent because it was discovered that he was a well-known playwright; and, indeed, that he was the author of one of the most popular wartime shows, a revue called *Razzle Dazzle* at Drury Lane Theatre. He was later promoted corporal, and ordered to found a magazine for the cadets of what was then called the Royal Flying Corps.

My life was changed by this. His success as a writer meant that, as a private, he was making considerably more money than a general. He took lodgings for my mother, younger sister and me in the Hampshire village of Hursley, conveniently near the KRRC barracks at Winchester, and we all lived well. In exchange for free tickets to Drury Lane, the officers granted my father generous leaves. The sergeants cleaned his brass, they became regular guests in our house, and joints of beef from the quartermaster's stores had a way of dropping through the manhole in our coal cellar.

For me, the upheaval in our family life, at the most impressionable age, awakened in me a taste for country life and country pursuits which has stayed with me ever since. Even as a little boy I knew, beyond a peradventure of doubt, that one day I intended to be a writer like my father, but if it had not been for the war we might simply have remained a family in suburban London, and I might have grown up a Cockney sparrow.

As it was, I was billeted with my sister in the cottage of a farm worker in deepest Hampshire. My parents occupied the schoolhouse nearby. For some reason, and I cannot imagine what that was, there wasn't room for us to be there with them. The cottage was called The Vine, after the grapevine which grew outside the front door. It was sandwiched between a splendid blacksmith's forge and a filbert tree up the road. I adored the forge; as did all the local dogs who collected there to chew the frogs which the smith carved out of the horses' hooves when he was shoeing them. My chewing place was the filbert tree up the road.

We were the lodgers of country folk, whose wages at that time were about fifteen shillings a week with a couple of piglets thrown in every six months. The cured pigs provided our main supply of meat, apart from illegally snared rabbits and, occasionally, an unwary pheasant. Our landlord was a remote person who lived in a vast mansion in a park, and appeared to own all the land as far as the eye could see in every direction. His name was Sir George

Cooper who had married, I later learned, a wealthy American heiress.

The only rather misty recollection I have of our then feudal squire is of seeing him, together with his wife, in his carriage and pair, driving in a stately way to church through the narrow street of Hursley. As he passed, we villagers were expected to press against the wall, touching our forelocks or removing our caps. I owe a lot to him. It was on his land, as a charge of one of his estate workers, that I began to learn the ways of the countryside. It was sheer heaven.

It was in Hursley that I made the first real friend in my life. He was a country boy named George Bennett; and if I was a Tom Sawyer, he was my Huckleberry Finn. We formed a friendship which has lasted to this day. We united, with some success, to defeat the other infant roughs in the village. One of our best ploys was to mix up mud and water in a bucket behind the wall where the nut tree grew. When the brew was made, I sat on the wall to taunt the other children passing by, and when I had attracted a goodly company I gave George the word and he shot the muddy water over the wall into the thick of them.

My father strongly disapproved of our behaviour. He declared that a particular field in which we used to go to play was out of bounds. He designated it 'The Ruffians' Field'. But his ban made it only the more deliciously attractive. It was a meadow which danced with butterflies; where there were mice and moles in every shifted piece of soil; where there were crab apple trees to climb, and where there was always an opportunity for a fight with the other village kids.

George and I hated these other kids, although I am sure that we were quite as beastly as they were. I remember seeing another boy climb a tree to take a squab pigeon out of the nest in his scout's hat, and kill it by squashing it into the ground; and I can still recall my fury when I found some of my enemies rolling naked baby mice down a steep slope, little things which they had hooked out of the nest. Even then, I suppose, I was sensitive to animal suffering. One day, during a wartime summer one of the swallows which nested under the eaves of my parents' schoolhouse hanged herself on a noose of hair which had strayed out of the nest. I cried and cried.

But I cannot pretend that I was not a hunter. George and I plagued the sticklebacks in Dog's Kennel Pond in Hursley Park. When they were gravid, and showed red, we called them redbreasts. We hunted out pheasants' nests. Once I found a nest which a rat had raided; there was only one egg which was left unbroken and it became my most cherished possession until my small sister dropped it. I haven't quite forgiven her yet.

I believe the strongest recollection I have of my childhood, which may have been one of the most influential, was picking up cartridge cases after a big shoot in Hursley Park. The sweet smell inside them of the burnt powder enchanted me more than the brass in the bases and the gay colours of the paper casings. They sent me on my way.

At last, my father sent me on my way too. He had tried to tame me in a Dame's school in Winchester, where George was also a pupil, then he decided that with the pressures of wartime I must be sent to a school where I would be subjected to proper discipline. At the age of seven I went to boarding school at Stonyhurst, under Pendle Hill in Lancashire. I got the discipline all right. Inside the prison of school, as it was then, I was unable to get my fist into the countryside again for years.

It was fortunate for me that during my time at Stonyhurst I developed pneumonia at a time when doctors knew little about it, and I nearly died. Fortunate, because it was determined that in my convalescence I must spend one term at home. The family had by then moved to a house at St Leonard's-on-Sea, part of Hastings. The war was well over. My father was fairly prosperous and I was able to renew my countryside education.

2

THE MAKING OF A COUNTRYMAN

The mystery of heredity and environment – my father and his elder brother – 'the most exciting thing that has happened to me in my life' – countryside adventures in East Sussex – Charles Scutt, the manager of the Gaiety Theatre at Hastings – Harry, the bathing attendant at Mrs Sageman's establishment at St Leonard's pier – a theory about brown hares and dormice – what Harry told me about fishing and his wife – how I beat the schoolmasters.

In any dispute on whether it is heredity or environment which makes a man what he is, I am undecided. I challenged the early Cockney environment in which I was brought up, yet I followed slavishly in my father's footsteps as an author and journalist. He was no countryman, although in different circumstances he might easily have been one. The urge was there; he was an eager back gardener, but opportunity denied him the richer sports of the field. In boyhood, I often thought that I saw a wistful look in his eye when he saw me packing my rods on the bar of my bicycle to go fishing. And I have never ceased regretting one day we had on a fairground together, when he bought me five shots with a rifle to shoot ping-pong balls floating up and down on a jet of water, and I pressed on after the game was over to the next sideshow. He just said, as we went on our way, 'I would have liked to have had a go myself.' I had shamefully denied him.

My eyes were opened by his elder brother, Lewis, a lion of a man, who on his occasional sorties from Africa to our little house in Hastings brought the veldt into our sitting-room. I would squat behind armchairs, hoping not to be noticed, while he talked, and how well he talked, of wild adventures in the bush, of the opening of the dark Continent; of days when the best things in life were fighting and hunting, drinking and feasting – and Lewis did not overlook the fifth.

He was the same man years later, when I was sitting at the communal table with him in one of the London clubs, who capped a conversation on the normally boring subject of 'the most exciting thing that has happened to me in my life'. There were several members present who had had more than a usual share of human experience. They told of war-time adventures, of following dangerous animals in jungles, of hot places, of assignments with exotic beauties in places hotter still. My uncle, looking back on his not uneventful career, proposed that the highest moment in a man's life was none of those things. The greatest, he said, was the unforgettable second when you felt the double-tug of a salmon and, when you lifted your rod point, he was on. It happened that most of the men sitting over the port were fishermen. Without demur, they agreed there was no experience to compare with that.

Long before, I was seduced by the call of the sirens of the streams and the waves and the green fields. While I know that heredity – and I don't care what any damned fool of a scientist or politician chooses to say – is of importance in the shape of the man to be, I readily recognise that environment, even if it cannot make you into someone else, can mould you into the shape you *want* to be. Oddly enough, the prevailing influence is seldom your nearest and dearest. Look at yourself. For most of us, in our most impressionable years, the people who moulded us were not primarily our parents, and emphatically not our school-teachers; but outsiders, sometimes quite extraordinary ones.

In my case, in those months when I was supposed to be too ill to go back to boarding school, I was blessed with the improbable friendship of two uncommon people. The first was the manager of the then Gaiety Theatre at Hastings. He was no ordinary theatre manager. His name was Charles Scutt; and he had the spare figure, the walnut-wrinkled nut-brown face of a man who had spent many years of his life in the Antipodes. In full evening dress, when Charles welcomed patrons outside the box-office of his seaside theatre, he quite often had a tame dormouse in his pocket, cuttings from his garden in his buttonhole, and a clutch of hard-boiled plovers' eggs, ready for his supper, in the pocket under his tails.

On Sundays he used to take me, with his son of my own age, on splendid walking expeditions into the countryside of East Sussex. It is incidental that he also kept open house for me in the stage box of the Gaiety, when the touring companies came round, twice a week during the summer, with a new play.

The great days were the hikes through Sussex marsh and Sussex gorse. We always went out with a purpose. In April, we searched the marshes for green plovers' eggs, the ponds for moorhens' nests. Boiled for tea, after a long day's march, these were the best eggs I have ever eaten. In high summer, after the cowslips were over, we explored for wild orchids and ferns for the garden. In autumn, in the fullness of the year, armed with crook sticks we filled baskets with blackberries; and, on great days, fell on a flush of field mushrooms.

But the passion of Charles Scutt's life was dormice; those delicious little creatures coloured like filberts, with boot-button eyes and fragile tails as beautifully bushed as a red squirrel's. In the twenties in East Sussex, along the hazel hedgerows, they were relatively common. Mr Scutt, as I always reverently addressed him, had a nose like a ferret for them. He could spot their round leafy nests, about the size of a cricket ball, in the arms of the nut trees. Carefully rolling back his sleeves, flexing his fingers like a piano player, he would ease his arms through the foliage to cup the nest in his hands. Again and again he trapped the mouse and her family, carefully knotting them up in his handkerchief.

At home, in his house named Thalassa on the cliffs over-looking Hastings, he had a large cage in the dining-room for his dormice. He kept some of them for years. In the wild, they are at best annuals. Mr Scutt's ambition was to breed from them. But although he frequently succeeded in tempting them to start a nest, and although he had them hand-tamed and as fat as butter, he never succeeded in his breeding plans. So far as I am aware, nobody ever has; and now dormice are as rare as kingfishers.

There is probably an answer. For years nobody succeeded in attempts to encourage the brown hare to breed in captivity. Kept in hutches, nothing ever happened. Then one day a couple of hares were introduced into a big cat cage which chanced to be empty, in the London Zoo. In their season they produced leverets. It was discovered that to perform their sexual display, hares need space to make their mad sexual antics in the air. Fortuitously provided with it, the coition worked.

I ought to add that I am not quite sure whether the London Zoo was the first place where hares were mated successfully in captivity. It may well have been the Munich Zoo. Sufficient to say that the discovery came about at approximately the same time. It would be pleasant to think that some zoologist might one day fluke on a way to propagate dormice; those enchanting harmless creatures, which are becoming so increasingly rare. Some years ago I offered five pounds to any keeper who could catch one for me. A lot of them said they were sure they could. I promised to donate the mouse to the children's section of the Natural History Museum. But no one brought me a dormouse.

The second friend who did so much to make me what I am I only knew as Harry. He was in charge of the changing huts at Mrs Sageman's bathing establishment, situated beside what was then St Leonard's Pier. We used to go there, the whole family of us, for our morning swim in the chilly tumultuous waters of the Channel. My father, who was plump and a powerful swimmer, revelled in it. I, who was skinny and a weak swimmer, loathed it. But it was a ritual we had to go through. We journeyed delightfully on the top of a yellow council tram, which reeled drunkenly down the London Road to Warrior Square and the front. There, carrying our bathing togs, we would see Mrs Sageman, the proprietress of the huts on our stretch of beach, upturned on her head, waggling her legs in the air as she performed like an overweight porpoise, issuing her invitation to us all to join her establishment wallowing in the briny. But it was Harry I always wanted to see.

Harry was built like the rocks I grew to love at low tide. He was an enormous man, or so I thought at the time, built out of ship's teak, coloured like mahogany, with a smile on his face which gleamed with white ivory. He also had a piratical gold ring in his ear. I never saw him except in a high-necked blue jersey. Theoretically, he was a mere bathing attendant, but for me he had all the glamour of Long John Silver himself.

He had a sea-chest on the front, heavily tarred and stuffed with magical things which, while I knew him, I never got to the bottom of. But if anything was ever wanted, Harry had it in his sea-chest. Looking back, I am sure that he was totally illiterate. But he was one of the wisest men I ever met.

He taught me the time-table of the tides. He showed me how to handle a big shrimping net; how to bait a gin with crab bait and lower it among the crevices in the rocks to lure prawns. When everybody else had gone home from the bathing beach, he would sit on his sea-chest weaving his nets – he was for ever making nets or knotting lines for something or other – and teach me how to dig for lugworms and sand-eels; how to lever out shore crabs with a hook on a pole to get them out of the crevices in the rocks; how to fight a conger or a dogfish; how to handle a seine net when the mackerel shoaled into the shallows.

'Wimmin,' he used to say, 'are always better prawners

than men. They're gentler when they put down and lift the gins.' And, 'remember, no conger is ever dead until the sun sets or the sun rises. If you touch him in between, he'll have a finger off yer.'

He had a trick he loved playing with me of pressing one of the tin moulds I had for making shapes in the sand into the low tidemark beyond the shingle. When he invited me to break up the sand mould I always knew that there would be a toy boat which he had made himself, often out of a walnut shell, inside it. How he introduced the boat into the mould, I never discovered. He was a magical man.

Again and again, he would sit with me until the sun went down, making things for me, showing me how to organise a ledger line, how important it was to know the proper way to bait a hook. When I saw him next morning to press on with my boyish enquiries, he would ask me what my mother had said when I came home so late. 'Nothing,' I would reply, never telling him that I thought that my father was a little jealous of the intimate relationship I had with the old salt. 'What about you?' Harry would grin. His comment was invariably, 'My old missus wasn't arf woild with me.'

With Harry's aid I equipped myself with a battery of prawning gins, which I baited with split crabs skewered into the base. I had a pole with a hook on the end to lower the gins into likely holes in the rocks. I got to know the pattern of the low tide rocks so well that I could walk out on them before the falling tide had uncovered them. First out got the best fishing. And, as I danced through the still hidden rocks, it gave me the diabolical pleasure that boys enjoy to hear frantic females screaming on the beach that I was about to be overwhelmed by the tide.

There was scarcely a day when I did not fall in. I couldn't have cared less with a full tin of fat prawns tied to my belt. In the neap tides, I could actually get beyond the necklace of rocks adjoining the shore and put my big shrimping net in virgin water. I picked up prawns, whiting, dabs and even eating crabs, as well as a bucketful of brown shrimps.

I flogged the prawns, oh dear, at sixpence a dozen, to a fishmonger on the front. The fishmonger sold them for a shilling. My father bought my crabs. I spent the money buying more gins at half-a-crown a time from Harry who, I recollect, once gave me a gin for nothing when my father lost his glasses in the sea. Harry recovered them at low tide and shared his tip with me. He was a wonderful friend.

I discovered myself in those halcyon months in the countryside, and beside the seaside with Harry. Although I was soon sent back to school, I was never seriously ill again. I never feared a schoolmaster again. I knew the way that I was going.

3

THE POACHING YEARS

My conception in a gamekeeper's cottage – love in a hop kiln –
shooting with danger – a cannonball of a cabbage – caged in the less
fashionable part of Kensington – poaching rabbits – a cottage of
my very own – my first shoot – my distinguished poaching friend
– John Buchan's gentlemen poachers – the use of a deer's leap and
'flywater only' – the story of a Wiltshire peasant – how I became
legitimate – how I was enlisted into war.

I fancy that my mother conceived me in a gamekeeper's
cottage in the thick of a covert at Tenterden in Kent. It
belonged to a hop farmer named Hukins, and in latter years
I only knew the place as a ruin. On sentimental journeys we
used to go there for picnics.

Hukins was a survivor of the nineteenth-century yeomen
farmers. He regarded everybody who invaded his land,
even his friends, as potential poachers. My mother told me
that in the years before I was born, he used to slap the men's
pockets to discover whether they had taken any pheasant's
eggs, and to smash them if they had. He littered his fields
with brambles and brush to defeat intruders who planned to
net his partridges. He had the peasant's suspicion when my
father acquired a greyhound called Proof. He was thinking
of his hares.

Years later, drawn to the place of which my father had so
many memories, I used to go to Tenterden in Kent at
hop-picking time to roast jacket-potatoes in the brimstone
fire in the oast house; and to sleep. How well I slept, in the
soporific embrace of the sack pockets in which the hops
were pressed.

I would take my gun to Tenterden. It was a weapon,
proofed only for black powder, which ought to have blown
up in my hands; I had inherited it from my grandfather.
Damascus-barrelled, with a slide to lock it under the

triggerguards, I had no business to be using it at all. Surprisingly, out of sheer habit, it held together. I used to sneak out with it at dawn to knock off rabbits – until Mr Hukins caught me. After that I never went back to his farm again.

But I was fascinated, I was always fascinated, by firearms. One Christmas my father gave me a pump air-gun. All we had for a shooting manor was a small back garden. I was denied any game for targets, except sparrows; and I was not very good at sparrow-shooting. But my eye was fixed on a monster target, a cannonball of a cabbage in the garden, for which my father had been awarded a 'highly-commended' in a local horticultural walkabout. It was irresistible. I put one slug after another into it, until the fatal day when it was brought into the kitchen. In terror I waited as the cabbage was served on the table. But nobody complained. It may be that we swallowed the lead slugs without noticing them. It may be that my mother got rid of them without comment. More likely my pump airgun was not as efficient as I thought it was.

I was far more successful with my fishing. The sea-fishing my father shared with me. He had a rowboat for a time, in which we brought back huge catches of plaice, dabs, flounders, weavers and dogfish. I caught cod off the pier, and bass in the breakers. I was a successful coarse fisherman in the reservoirs about Alexandra Park. But it was after my father's days were over, when we were enclosed in a little flat in the less fashionable part of Kensington, that I found myself tied to an office desk and struggling like a caged bird to find the countryside again.

I somehow found the money to buy a .22 Browning Repeating Rifle at Gamages. I still have it; and it is worth far more money now than I paid for it in 1930. With a friend who had no rifle, but a car with a sunshine roof, I used to go on poaching excursions after rabbits. Our hunting ground was a heath outside Leatherhead and, night after night, shooting in the headlights, we would knock off forty or fifty rabbits. Nobody ever challenged us. I suppose at that time we were culling vermin that needed to be got rid of. And with the little rifle, we weren't making much noise.

There were few opportunities for me of legitimate sport in those days. I once had a chance, at a covey of partridges with a 12-bore magnum, but I missed with both barrels and split my lip on the recoil. I was a neophyte. If I had been brought up differently I might, at the age of twenty, have distinguished myself in the field. As it was, I had to learn it all later. I meant to learn it.

Some time in my late twenties I rented a weekend cottage outside Midhurst in Sussex. It was a simple little place with no light except oil lamps and no heat except the wood I could garner for the open fire. But there I found my gumbooted feet. I began to garden. I adopted a fledgling jackdaw and, like Barnaby Rudge, provided him with a basketwork cage for his sleeping quarters. I went to bed serenaded in their season by nightingales (there was a wood nearby where the nightingales were so numerous that BBC radio, all there was at the time, had wired it for sound). By day, I had the drumming of the snipe, the weeping call of the peewits and, at dusk, the cry of the bats. I was young enough then for my ears to pick up the high squeak of their calls. I bred mallard, which I launched on to the cattle pond in front of the little farmhouse. I got ferrets, a dog and two jills, and learnt how to work them.

The first shooting I had was over a marsh nearby about which, in a laboured handwriting, the tenant farmer, on the thinnest possible legal grounds, awarded me the wildfowl shooting which was 'my rights'. I think he was a gypsy. He once told me that in his younger years, he and his wife had made a living trapping song birds and caging them for the market. I paid his rent by giving him a share of the wild duck, the snipe, the rabbits and the occasional game bird which I shot.

The risk, without benefit of game licence, and only the

most doubtful right to shoot at all, added zest to the chase. In the panoply of big shoots, as a guest on subsequent occasions when I was perhaps the only gun without a hook to my name, it was never quite the same thing. I liked being an outlaw, and I make no apology for it. After my sport assumed complete respectability, I pursued it over the years with decreasing interest. Now, although I am as fascinated as ever by the sport of it, most of the time I prefer not to shoot at all.

The philosophy of it was summed up for me years ago when a dashing naval officer said to me, 'There's nothing in this world to compare with an August partridge and a September pheasant.' He had indeed ordered his whole life on that principle. In his youth, in command of a primitive submarine in the First World War, he had driven it into the Dardanelles and sunk two Turkish battleships. For that, he was awarded the Victoria Cross. He conducted the rest of his life in the same piratical spirit. Women adored Commander Holbrook, RN.

I had another friend who wrote the classic *History of Firearms*. His name was Major Hugh B. C. Pollard and, since like Commander Holbrook he is now dead, there is no need to disguise the fact that throughout most of his career he was involved in what is called 'the cloak and dagger business'. He applied it on his own more splendid place near mine, where he owned about ten acres ringed with the great estates on which they were rearing tens of thousands of pheasants a year. One season, with scientific precision and a vast knowledge of the ways of pheasants, he planted one of his fields with dredge corn. I have no doubt that he also employed aniseed with effective skill.

None of his family were allowed to approach his home reserve. At last he issued an invitation – I was one of the guns – for the great shoot. We turned in the dogs. I doubt if I have seen so many pheasants take wing at the same time. For a couple of minutes, with two guns, it was the shoot of a lifetime. After that, it was all over. The birds, hundreds at a time, hustled back into their home coverts. Hugh was grimly satisfied with his poaching adventure.

The classic fiction of gentlemen poachers is John Buchan's story *John Macnab*. In it he tells how a trio of men, all of them rich and successful, are overwhelmed with the ennui of fame and fortune. They are all country sportsmen. In search of the refreshment of pure excitement, they issue a challenge to three Highland estates that they will poach two takeable stags and a salmon within a given period. Under the pseudonym of John Macnab, they undertake to smuggle the beasts and the fish beyond the boundaries of the chosen estates, returning them with a suitable reward for charity if the bet is won. All law and order is organised against them. But John Macnab nearly wins. The story ends, as a Buchan story would, with everybody shaking hands on the adventure. A book written more than fifty years ago it is obviously dated, but it is still tremendous fun.

A lot of poaching, in my experience, consists in extending the complicated game laws. None of us would wish to defend the people, townspeople mostly, who trespass on estates with cars and miniature rifles. But few of us haven't at some time over-exercised our rights. There is a feudal law, for instance, which lays down that you are entitled to pick up a head of game which has fallen not more than 'a deer's leap' beyond your own boundary. 'A deer's leap', in practice, is a very elastic definition.

Another rule, which I have broken in practice if not in theory, is that one in angling, 'flywater only'. I remember fishing on a chalk stream in Wiltshire in which all the most aldermanic trout gathered under a bridge by the roadside. I was told that they would not touch a fly because the people looking over the bridge regularly fed them with bread. I hunted in my flybox for the biggest white artificial moth I could find. Casting upstream, as a dry fly purist should, I put my moth over the neb of one of the best of them. I had him at the first cast.

I have fond memories of fishing with A. G. Street on the Helmsdale in Sutherland, which is strictly fly only. It was one of those days when the surface of the water glittered with steely indifference, and the fish stuck dourly on the bottom like iron bars. We were both exasperated by our failure to awaken any interest in any of them. At last, under a clay bank, Arthur and I spotted a fish lounging somnolently in the mud.

'Listen,' Arthur said, 'I am not a gentleman. I am a Wiltshire peasant. I am going to have that fish.'

He moved his heavy bulk down the bank, crossing one of those trembling swing bridges which on Highland rivers are calculated to unnerve a monkey. But Arthur was determined. On the other side of it, he got me to point out where his fish was lying. Then he produced a fly as large as a pony shoe out of his book. He sank it slowly beside the fish and, with a hoot of triumph, foul-hooked it. It played as uncomfortably as foul-hooked fish do. Arthur had it on for a few minutes before it slipped him.

It was lucky that he lost it. Out of the empty bowl of the Highland landscape, in which you could have believed that there wasn't another human being within miles, the factor appeared with his telescope under his arm. In the Highlands, however lonely it may seem, only a fool will believe that someone isn't always looking.

The years that followed were all coloured by my first poaching experiences at that weekend cottage in West Sussex. At last my landlords, the Cowdray Estate, no doubt exasperated by my depredations which must have been known to them, offered me a rough shoot in thick woodland between Midhurst and Fernhurst. I could just afford the rent. From that time on I became legitimate. I was even invited to shoot as a guest on the great estate.

In 1938 I met Robert Churchill, the gunmaker. I wrote an article about him in the then newly-founded *Picture Post*. I little dreamt, when he built my first good gun for me, that thirty years later I would write his biography; and become a beneficiary in his will. I little guessed that I would be the writer of the standard textbook *Churchill's Gameshooting*.

I tried out Churchill's gun for the first time in Verdley Wood, outside Midhurst, shooting partridges by myself on the day that World War II broke out. It was strange that the outbreak of two world wars, the Kaiser's and Hitler's, should have come at such climacteric moments in my own country life. And on that morning of 3rd September 1939, I had no idea, like everybody else, what was going to happen next. I assumed that I would soon be in uniform. Walking over the stubble, I savoured all the memories of my past. It was mostly smells – the perfume of a newly-fired cartridge, the fragrance of fresh-caught fish, the strangely parallel smell of beer and intimate female. Just as I had my boots firmly pressed into the fullness of country life, I was about to be uprooted.

In fact, for me it did not turn out quite as I expected. I was enlisted as a war correspondent. I had what was called a lucky war. But from 1939 until now, I can find no developing pattern in my sporting life, if pattern there was. I had arrived where I wanted to go.

4

SPORTING IN WARTIME

How British corps artillery winged a German partridge – why war correspondents carried guns – a disreputable engagement with a flock of geese – an engagement with an imaginary U-boat which depth-charged a shoal of fish – the mayfly season which interfered with the Normandy landings – the Second World War commemorated with Ragged Robin – London Airport as a partridge manor – the man who married John D. Rockefeller's daughter – salmon in food-rationed Britain – the importance of knowing a Reverend Mother – the art of passing Customs on parboiled beef – the discomforts of wearing women's lingerie.

After we had crossed the Rhine in 1945, I joined the first battle fought by the British army on German soil. We advanced in extended order, the infantry sandwiched in rows between a long line of tanks. The medium guns were planted on our flanks. The heavies threw their stuff over our heads. All hell let loose.

As we marched over the terrain, I recognised at once that we were in ideal partridge country. The land was lined with roots and kale. Sure enough, in what must have been one of the biggest drives in history, a strong covey broke just in front of me. I saw one bird fall. Breaking ranks I went after him. He was a strong runner, and without a dog I had a lot of trouble catching up with him. I think that I can truthfully say that the war stopped for a bit while I ran crazily through the roots to pick him. I even forgot the thunder of the guns.

When the battle was over I despatched my bird with a message to corps artillery. I hoped they would be gratified to learn that on a day in which I understood they had expended five hundred tons of high explosive, they had at least winged one German partridge.

It is fashionable to take the attitude that everything in war is awful but any old soldier knows that the laughs have always balanced the horrors. I was only a bogus soldier. As

37

a war correspondent, my job was to look for trouble without taking an active part. Theoretically, according to the Convention, we were not supposed to be armed, but in practice I think most of us carried a gun. In that war of movement we knew what our fate would be, since most of us would be instantly recognised if we were taken prisoners. Personally, I felt happier with a pistol in my belt.

Without dwelling on unpleasant details, the gun served me well to put wounded horses and cattle out of their misery during the Normandy landings. But I also used it for sport. Although it is terribly difficult to use an automatic pistol with any accuracy, I practised on beer bottles until I got reasonably efficient. My proudest shot was during the British occupation of a village, when a rabbit bolted from a patch of scrub. I dropped him in full run, and provided a dinner for the chaps who were with me; they were members of the Wessex Division.

Not all my sporting adventures in the war were reputable. One day when I was going into the forward areas, my colleagues in the War Correspondents' mess, knowing my proclivities, asked me if, as a change from a diet of bully beef, I could loot them some chickens. In the no-man's-land between the two sides, in the deserted farmsteads, there were plenty of fowls if you could catch them. I couldn't. These chickens, as soon as they saw anybody in battledress, however much he whistled disinterest, scrambled up the nearest rampart, and you could not get after them without revealing yourself in a field of machinegun fire. But I discovered a flock of geese, and I broke my penknife trying to slaughter the first. When I had at last killed them all and loaded them into my jeep for my hungry colleagues, I was covered from top to tail with feathers. A soldier looking like one out of a Giles wartime cartoon, climbed out of a slit trench and said to me balefully, 'Them was laying eggs.'

I make no excuse for my conduct at that time. The lily-hearted have no place in the ruthlessness of war. What we were concerned with was survival. But it never lacked its grim fun.

I was aboard an old destroyer at the time of Dunkirk when the radar signalled a U-boat. We heaved over a salvo of dustbin depth charges. All that showed on the surface was a vast harvest of fish. It was a shoal of fish, not a U-boat, which had shown on our radar screen. We, too, stopped the war for a bit, to put out the ship's boats and bring the catch into the galley.

My uncle, Major Lewis Hastings, who I have mentioned already, was the BBC's military commentator on the radio. Many will remember him for prophesying that we wouldn't open the second front, the invasion of Europe, until the mayfly season on the trout rivers had begun. No fisherman would ever stand for it, he said. In fact, he was dead right. The Normandy landings began on 6th June 1944.

On the day the great news broke out that the Allies had landed in France, and every road in the South of England was blocked with soldiers and armour on their way to Europe, it is told that an angler fishing off a bridge in Wiltshire held up a division while he fought the biggest trout he had hooked in his life. 'This will never happen to me again,' he said. 'You must wait.'

I have so many memories of the blitz, which wasn't nearly as unhappy as people today who didn't experience it will tell you that it was. For a start, only the people you didn't want to know ran away from London. Wild flowers grew again on the bomb sites. If we were going to have a flower, like the Flanders poppy, to commemorate the Second World War, I knew that I would choose Ragged Robin, which proliferated wherever the bombs fell. And I have never got over my astonishment that throughout the blitz in London, invaded as the city always is in winter with hundreds of thousands of migrant starlings, not one dead bird was ever picked up. When I was reporting the blitz, two dead pigeons in one night landed at my feet, but neither of them had been hurt by shell splinters. From the blood on their beaks it was evident that they were victims of avian tuberculosis.

My job, as the war correspondent of *Picture Post*, was different from most, especially from those reporting to the national newspapers. I had to get back from the various areas of war to bring the pictures to the office, and sometimes I was even able to take time off for fishing and shooting. They were easily come by for most of the men were elsewhere.

I have nostalgic memories of a day after partridges on a two-hundred-acre holding specialising in market gardening, on which we killed a hundred brace of birds. It is now the centre of London Airport; that same place in which it is recorded that a generation earlier, the great cricketer W. G. Grace was one of the followers when a pack of Bassett hounds killed a leveret. The hares and the partridges are still there among the runways of Heathrow, but now nobody can get near them.

During the war, I had the shooting over an estate at Bagnor, near Newbury. It was prolific in game; but I recall it chiefly for a brief conversation I had when I first met its then owner. He was a charming old Irishman named Armagh Saunderson. I suppose that I must have said something about somebody being very rich because the subsequent conversation went like this:

'It always makes me laugh a little,' said Armagh, 'when I hear of someone who is said to be very rich.'

'Why?' I asked.

'Did you ever hear of John D. Rockefeller?'

'Yes, who hasn't?'

'I married his daughter.'

'Was it worth it?'

'No.'

Thus ended the conversation. At about the same time,

another very rich man, if not as rich as John D. Rockefeller, invited me to fish for a week in early May, the best season of the year, on one of the best beats on one of the best rivers in Scotland. I had incredible luck. I killed about sixteen salmon, none of them weighing less than fifteen pounds. In those times of food rationing I naturally hoped that my host would present me with a fish, but when he saw me off on the train south there was no sign of it. At last, just as the train was drawing out, he remarked, 'Oh, by the way, the fish are in the luggage van.' I felt relief.

At King's Cross, the guard came to see me to enquire what I wanted done about the fish. I said that I could collect. 'They want a lot of collecting,' he said. My host had sent me home with every fish I had caught.

In wartime London it was virtually impossible to get a taxi. I was stuck with about two hundred and fifty pounds of fresh salmon in the early hours of the morning on an unwelcoming station. I forget how I did find a taxi in the end, but I bribed the driver with one of my fish if he carried me to Billingsgate, where I knew a dealer who would cure my catch.

At a time when the best you could normally buy was Spam or whalemeat, I was able to give my friends sides of smoked salmon, and we dined on it at home until we could scarcely bear the sight of it any more. You can have too much of any good thing.

Many of the restrictions were strange during the war. For example, it was illegal, I can't think why, to bring home fresh salmon from Southern Ireland. I had killed two fish in Connemara, on the waters of none other than Lord Killanin who now, God help him, is in charge of the Olympic Games. When I arrived back at London Airport, the Customs officer asked what I had got in 'those basses' and, on hearing, reminded me that it was illegal to export fresh salmon. 'They are a present,' I said, 'for my aunt, Mother Hastings, who is the Reverend Mother at the Sacred Heart

Convent in Hammersmith. The Customs officer crossed himself. He passed me on with the valedictory, 'Ask her to pray for me.' I am ashamed to say that my aunt never saw the colour of the salmon.

I was never ashamed that on my periodical returns from the war I brought in, whenever I could, great rolls of parboiled beef, which was then easily come by in the devastated areas of Normandy. It had to be parboiled to pass Customs and the meat shown to be free of germs. Indeed, the Customs officers got to know me so well that they would tell me what I had got before I even declared it.

There was an occasion when I was a smuggler. On one of the war fronts, from a bombed shop, I had looted a collection of women's silk underwear. It looked so flimsy that I decided to put it all on under my battledress. You must remember that at that time, girls' gew-gaws were unobtainable. I came home on a naval torpedo boat and have never been so close to heat exhaustion in my life. Women's clothes, especially if you've got on half-a-dozen sets of lingerie, are suffocating. By the time I had cleared Customs I must have shed ten pounds in sweat. But, as the French say, '*Vive le sport*'.

5

OUR COMIC OPERA SHOOT

The happiest shooting seasons of my life – the early morning drinker – the lethal bullet in a shotgun cartridge – the best and the worst dog in the world – the sows who ate my partridges – the day the model girls came to our shoot – the pheasant who roosted in the environs of Harrods – how Joad of The Brains Trust, and von Ribbentrop of the Nazi Party, upset the locals – the albino pheasant.

Shortly after Hitler's war when we discarded our battle-dresses (still worn, incidentally, including the gas capes, until quite ten years later by our beaters), a group of us took a rough shoot of about fifteen hundred acres on the Berkshire Downs at Compton. They were the happiest shooting seasons of my life. We stood on no ceremony. We were not interested, after the discipline of the war years, in being regimented again. We went shooting to enjoy ourselves. The bag was far less important than the outrageous fun of it all.

We invited all our friends to walk the Downs who had the legs for it. One of our guests, a very early riser who had the art of getting the back door of our lonely pub open at eight in the morning, sailed into battle, with about four pints under his belt, at 10 am. He shot with such immaculate timing that he was always able to raise his hat and say 'good morning' before pulling down any carrion who flew within anything less than extreme range of him. He specialised in crows.

There was another, Robert Churchill, the gunmaker, who liked to waste cartridges shooting at impossibly high pigeons. When I asked him what he thought he was up to, he explained cheerfully that once he started, all the other guns had a bang as well. 'Every time they fire, it's sixpence in my pocket.'

In those years of rationing, cartridges for a long time were difficult to get hold of. Churchill came to our rescue with ammunition which he labelled, as it turned out appropriately, 'Hercules'. He had made a lot of money selling cartridges to the RAF, loaded with a solid slug to train recruits in the practice of shooting down dive-bombers. When the war was over he bought the residue of his cartridges back from the Air Ministry, at a suitable discount, and reduced the lead slugs into small shot. Inevitably, some cartridges were overlooked and passed into circulation with the solid bullet still in them.

We had a taste of it on our shoot. On one of our days when we were walking through roots, a cock pheasant curled back high over my own head; he was a screamer. I was astonished when I shot, as was every other gun in the line, as the head parted from the body and the carcass bounded to earth in two pieces. And there was another incident when a farmer neighbour of ours shot at a hare at extreme range, but fortunately well behind the line of guns. To our surprise he killed it stone dead. When the dog retrieved it, it was so hard hit that it was not worth picking up.

We had fun with our dogs. A. G. Street rang me one day to ask if he might bring his new Labrador with him. 'I have just paid one hundred and fifty for him,' he said, 'and he is the best gundog I have ever had.' He added, in passing, that he had cannily written him off twenty-five per cent in the farm books already.

When I heard that this paragon of a dog was joining our shooting party, I told James Robertson Justice about it. 'If Arthur is bringing the best dog in the world', he replied, 'I'll bring the worst.' They were both in their way right.

On the great day, James turned up in his vintage yellow Rolls, with a hooded peregrine falcon on the back of the passenger seat and Friday, as the brute was called, sitting beside him. Friday was a brown German pointer with yellow eyes that flashed like a tiger's at bay. When James disembarked his huge bearded frame from his dreadnought of a car, we were intrigued to observe that he had rigged his belly with a sheet of cord spliced at the end with a strong piece of catapult elastic. We moved off to walk the partridges and James attached the dog's collar to the elastic. He then unwound himself out of a coil of fifty yards of cord. The pointer ranged out until, with a sharp jerk, James sprang him back on his haunches. Friday then raced wildly up and down the line of guns. What was supposed to be walking up partridges degenerated into a sort of skipping match.

Surprisingly, some of us actually shot some birds. But if they dropped within the limits of Friday's lunging rein, he ate them; reminding me of a time when at a rather more pompous partridge shoot, I was placed at a numbered stand in a field with a herd of sows. I shot rather well for me, dropping about seven brace. We picked up only about three as the sows had the rest before I could get to them.

I learnt long ago that it is no use making excuses to the head keeper, who in this instance knew that I had had a good stand. I handed over my little bag in silence, just hoping that he noticed the grins on the faces of those execrable pigs.

James's apologia for his awful dog was that Friday was quite all right when he was out on his own grouse hawking in the wilder parts of Sutherland. But if he had unhooded the peregrine sitting moodily in his old Rolls, I suspect the bird could have told a different story.

One of our more spectacular and glamorous shoots occurred when one of the glossy fashion magazines asked if they could send down some of their model girls to be photographed with the guns in the latest female sporting attire. The girls each had several outfits to wear for the photographer. And the day was enlivened when anybody who had downed a bird was liable to flush a dolly bird changing her clothes in the rough.

I have had the embarrassment, when we were counting the bag at the end of the day, to have a pheasant fly out of my game bag on to the roof of a neighbouring cottage. But I think Colonel Peter Fleming, the author, had the most exasperating experience of that sort. Driving to London, a pheasant crashed through his windscreen into the back seat of his car. Cursing the bird, but thankful for the small mercy that he had won a pheasant, he put the cock into the boot.

Back at his house in the West End of London, the door-bell was pushed by a suspicious policeman who asked if the car was his. When Peter said that it was, the policeman then got out his notebook and asked how his windscreen had been smashed. He implied that it had better be a good story; and the London officer was quite unimpressed by the story of the pheasant. 'All right, I'll prove it to you' said Peter.

He opened the boot of his car, and with indignant squawks of 'cock-up, cock-up' the pheasant took off and went to roost in the plane trees of a fashionable London Square.

Our most alarming guest was the radio philosopher of the time, Professor C. E. M. Joad of The Brains Trust. He invited himself again and again to our shoot, so eventually we agreed he might come. An obliging hare sat up on her hindquarters for him and permitted him to shoot about five times without moving. At last puss lolloped off, without a fleck of fur in disarray.

At our picnic lunch, I was mildly suspicious when Joad laid his gun beside him on a straw bale. Picking the gun up, I found it cocked and loaded. I took out the cartridges, and in silence I handed them back to him. Without a flicker of his beard he carefully loaded the gun again.

We did not ask him the next time. We wouldn't have dared, even if we had wanted to. The whole country seemed to know within hours who our guest had been, and what had happened. I became the most unpopular shooting man in Berkshire since the late Lord Iliffe of Yattendon, who had invited the German ambassador to one of his great shoots. His name was von Ribbentrop.

On our very last shooting day, and almost with the last shot, one of us killed a pure white cock pheasant. I belonged to a noisy luncheon club at that time, most of us writers, actors, and many of us shooting men, which was called The Thursday Club, and I had the bird mounted to decorate our table with an inscription on the plinth: TO THE OLD COCKS OF THE THURSDAY CLUB. We honoured it until its tail fell off. I think that some of our members must have given it too much to drink.

6

THE GOOD OLD DAYS

Shooting is not a destroyer of game – culling is essential to preserve the species – the origins of gameshooting – the ten best shots in England – the times when a shooting invitation meant packing a dinner jacket – 'Norfolk Liars' – shooting as an amateur profession – the days when pheasants were presented in bouquets – killing in thousands – Bob Churchill's last pheasant.

My son persists in asking me to write about 'the good old days' in the shooting field. And in my generation, I used to ask the old boys to tell me about the great days of their own youth. The past always seems to have been better. But in truth, I am inclined to think that the pattern of shooting today is healthier than it has ever been. The sport is more expensive but less exclusive. The new generation is more conscious of the importance of conservation. Vermin are not what they used to be.

Shooting, contrary to the opinion of some, has never been a destroyer. Any keeper knows that a good gun who can drop the leading pair out of a covey of partridges is doing the manor a good turn. Killing the old birds will spread the family over the estate. It is the best way of mixing up the young birds to reduce incestuous and sterile relationships. Indeed it is true that a partridge place, if not well shot, will soon have no partridges.

You will never persuade the 'antis', as they are called, to understand this. I was attacked on television once, when I talked about shooting stags in the Highlands of Scotland. People wrote to me protesting about what seemed to them a horrible sport. They commented on how happy the deer were in Windsor and Richmond Parks. They little knew that to preserve the herd in those Arcadian areas, the verderers have to go round in Land Rovers and knock off the old stags to give the youngsters a chance. Otherwise, no

A SALMON FISHER'S DREAM: About two hundred fish show in this remarkable picture taken from Galway Bridge. When the water is low they can be seen crowding into a three-foot deep rocky channel waiting to run upstream to spawn.   (see *Fishing in Ireland*)

It was a breach of the Geneva Convention for war correspondents, as I was, to be armed. But it was on the whole safer, and I mostly used my gun for sporting.

WAR . . . : In a situation like this, the taking of the burning town of Argentan during the Normandy campaign, nobody waited to find out if you were a non-combatant. I just ran. But there were other happier moments. (see *Sporting in Wartime*)

deer. In fact the big game hunter, supposedly the enemy of conservation, is the animals' best friend. Looking for a trophy of horn, he is killing a beast which is best out of the way. The old bull is a nuisance in the family.

I doubt whether in previous generations in Britain, people thought the way we do now. It never occurred to them that sports like bull-baiting and dogfighting and cockfighting were cruel. In the good old days, sporting was rough.

The Victorians, whatever you think of them, introduced humanitarianism. Paradoxically they also introduced, with the coming of the double-barrelled breechloader, a new method of shooting. Previously the capture of game had been with nets and shooting, such as it was, consisted in killing game on the ground. The invention of the breech-loader changed all that.

Driven gameshooting undoubtedly started in Norfolk, and a polished shooting code had been reached by the end of the nineteenth century. Guns were efficient, and after the black powder age the new smokeless powders allowed you to see what you were shooting at. This was the time in which the great shots of the Victorian era rose to fame.

It was customary then to name the ten best shots in England. Lord de Grey (later Marquis of Ripon) was always named as the first, and certainly he was one of the outstanding performers of the new school of shooting. De Grey, who gave up keeping a detailed list of the game he killed after 1913, bagged between 1867 and 1895, 316,699 head – including 111,190 pheasants – 89,491 partridges and 47,668 grouse. Before his death his score had been brought up to over half a million.

Nobody today would wish to have such a record. Surely nobody would want to be included among the five guns, listed in Hugh Gladstone's *Shooting Records*, who killed 6,493 rabbits at Blenheim in a day. None of them, it seems, had a sore shoulder.

My son, who argues that 'fings ain't what they used to be' has a point. It is true that the world in which they used to say 'up goes a sovereign, bang goes twopence, down comes half-a-crown', has passed. The great days of two-gun shooting are probably on the way out. The remnant of them still remains on great estates, but the syndicate shoot has taken graciousness and hospitality out of the field. A shooting party, alas, is now seldom a country house party.

I have had my share of the great days. I enjoyed the back end of the times when a shooting invitation meant packing your dinner jacket as well as your tweeds; when the ladies joined the guns for a luncheon of steak and kidney pudding (traditionally) in the shooting lodge; when it was seemly for your loader to be seen carrying a five-hundred round oak cartridge magazine, bound in leather of the correct London finish, with your initials stamped into the hide of it. It was proper to make sure that your pigskin cartridge bags (Payne-Gallwey model) and your guncase did not look too new. 'The Right Sort', as the Badminton Library described them, affected a well-worn air. 'The Wrong Sort' wore and carried all the new things. There was nothing which was socially more acceptable in the shooting field than a very old hat. One celebrated Victorian shot wore one which he had made out of a hedgehog.

Interestingly enough, it was not thought bad manners in Victorian times for a shooter to count, in the Continental style, how many head of game he felled. Nearly all of them carried what came to be called 'Norfolk Liars'; markers, some of them very elaborate, which ticked up the numbers of pheasants, partridges, rabbits and hares that the gun shot during the day. It was Sir Ralph Payne-Gallwey, the same man who invented the cartridge bag with an ever-open mouth, who had a marker introduced into the forehand of his guns. Every time he killed he made another flick. Whether it was thought improper then to report the score at the end of the day, is something which I have never discovered. Perhaps they kept the information, as Lord Walsingham did, for their game books. But Walsingham, like Colonel Peter Hawker, published his score in the end.

Those men who made such colossal bags of game were rich men, who paradoxically made an amateur profession of shooting. Every season they filled their diaries with the dates when they would shoot with each other. It was Lord Harris, I think, who refused to captain England at cricket because he had a date to shoot grouse in Yorkshire. They each let off ten to twenty thousand rounds in a season and they were good shots because the secret of straight shooting is constant practice and a knowledge from long experience of the game.

I used to laugh at my friend Robert Churchill when he instructed me that it does not matter at all if you miss the first six birds which come over you. 'You must run yourself in,' he'd say. I reminded him that in the company I normally kept, six birds is all you would see in a day. But Bob had lived through a lush Victorian period; used to the sort of day when, to use his own expression, 'bouquets' of pheasants flew over the guns on every drive.

No doubt some of the reputations of 'the ten best shots in England' rested on the sheer quantity of pheasants which were driven over them. They could pick the birds which suited them. I have been told that King George V, counted among the top shots of his time, always took the same bird in the same place. There were enough of them put over him to make a selection.

I was standing next to A. G. Street to watch him on a big shoot knock down about nineteen pheasants in a row. He took them all in the same place in the air, and at the pick-up it was seen that they had all dropped in a thirty-foot circle.

Those were the tail end of days which I suppose will never come again. I have happy memories of shooting with Cecil Hurlock at Woodbridge in Suffolk, where the game larder, a separate building, had an admirable range of two-fanged neck hooks to accommodate two thousand brace of pheasants. I remember that on Lord Iliffe's place at Yatten-don in Berkshire, they had a sort of game counter fixed on a box with knotted string, which marked every ten brace brought into the game cart. The shooting lodge, in the thick of the coverts – it is still there – was large enough to house a family.

My own latterday memories of the great days are largely fixed on rather odd ones. I cannot forget when William Hill the bookmaker kindly asked me to shoot with him. A butler, with a dumb waiter, brought us drinks at our stands. On another occasion I was asked shooting in the potato fields of Lincolnshire. In that flat part of country the birds were not very good, although they were plentiful; but the charm of the experience was that the guns were carried from stand to stand on a miniature railway, which had been installed to move the potatoes to make the crisps.

I recollect another more testing shoot on the Iliffe estate. A great day had been planned when the Duke of Gloucester, himself a first class shot with 16-bore guns, was to have been the honoured guest. But the big day in November was completely blotted out by fog. Not a shot was fired. An army of pheasants was ranging about to the delight of every poacher in Reading. In January, the estate asked a lot of us to help clear them up. It is the only time in my life that I have stood in two banks of guns. None of us had ever tackled birds who flew like it. You had to shoot, as one of the other guns said to me, before you saw them. We got a reasonable bag, but there were two thousand birds who were too good for us.

Looking back, I am reminded of the latter days of Robert Churchill, when 'bouquets' of pheasants were passing over him and he didn't raise his gun. I asked him why he was not shooting. He made a grimace and said, 'Too much steak and kidney pud for lunch.' In truth, Bob had shot his last pheasant; although on his deathbed, he insisted on having his gun beside him, saying, 'Keep the window open, there is going to be a helluva battue in a minute'. Not unlike the poacher in one of Eden Philpotts's one-act plays who, as he was dying, asked for his gun. Out of the window from his bed, he knocked off a right-and-left at one of his hated neighbour's carrier pigeons. He passed away, a happy man.

Not all the shoots I have been to have been a success. I remember a group of us being asked by a great industrialist to shoot over land which belonged to his firm. He assured us that it ought to be pretty good. We equipped ourselves for the great day with two guns each and a few hundred cartridges. In the event, we walked miles over barren fields. I seem to recall that the total bag was two pheasants and an unsuspecting rabbit.

7

GREAT SHOTS

If you shoot enough you can be a first class shot – it costs money to acquire muscle memory – the performance of a man of eighty – Lord Dorchester's seventy grouse in a stand – Lord Rank and A. G. Street in the field – an encounter with Royalty – an encounter with a cad – Henry Williamson and the dragonfly – a thousand dead birds in the field – twenty to one on the old cock – 'Five hundred pheasants before luncheon, sir, or no grace birds for you' – shooting our host's birds for him.

The men who fired ten thousand rounds a season in Victorian and Edwardian times achieved a consistency of performance at driven game which is unlikely, probably fortunately, ever to be achieved again. I had a brief taste of what can be done with constant practice under the direction of Robert Churchill. When we were going shooting together, he would invite me on the day before to come to his clay shooting grounds at Crayford in Kent.

'See how quickly you can get through two hundred rounds,' he would say. Firing a pair of guns over two double traps, with Churchill himself loading for me, I settled into a rhythm of instinctive and balanced shooting. He did better than throw over 'tall pheasants'. He offered me 'low partridges' starting at about fifteen yards. With every double shot, he ordered me to take a pace forward. In the end, until I got too tired, I was taking right-and-lefts at clays, just cutting over the top of a hedge, at a distance of about seven yards.

I often felt that it was no credit to me that when we arrived at the real shooting field I was almost too effective. Briefly, in the vigour of youth, I had become a sort of professional. Now, I am happy to say, I am as scrappy a shot as the next man. I was never a born shot. Greatness for a short period – one in which I was writing about 'how to shoot straight' – was thrust upon me.

I mention the matter only because long experience in the shooting field has taught me that anybody who trains like an athlete can gain himself the reputation of being a first class shot. It is not really very difficult. You just have to learn to point your gun with the same fluency and certainty that you would point your index finger at any moving target. The index finger, married as it must be to your eye, is never wrong. If you press the trigger of your gun on first aim you won't miss. It is merely a matter of practice to learn to use a gun like an extension of your own arm.

The trouble, of course, is that it costs a lot of money, especially these days, to pay for the cartridges and get into the habit of shooting. That is the main reason why top shots are not as common as they used to be. They have not got the finance to acquire 'muscle memory'.

I name Archie Coats, that remarkable performer who shot wood-pigeons professionally for many years, as one of the few people left in our times who can shoot with the same deadly precision as the Victorians like Lord Walsing-ham, Payne-Gallwey, Stonor and the rest who are listed in the sporting records.

While I have watched Archie Coats shoot with admira-tion, my own memories are largely of men who were clearly born shots. They may have had to practise, but they shot with a certain insouciance which suggested that they had never really had to try to master the game. I recollect watching an old boy of over eighty, as stiff on his pins as boys of over eighty must be, shooting partridges at Yatten-don. His swing was inevitably limited. But, shooting par-tridges, he killed nineteen in a row in front. Then, as the beaters came out, they flushed a lone red leg. He had him too, making his score twenty for the drive.

Lord Dorchester, in his sporting reminiscences, tells how he had seventy grouse in a stand, all made more exciting because in the heat of the shooting he ran out of cartridges. His loader had to run two stands up the line to replenish his ammunition. Otherwise, he believed he would have killed a hundred birds to his own gun. He was one of the latter great shots, and I do not doubt that he could have achieved it. But in my heart I think more of people like A. G. Street, who was cursed with a club foot and a lock in his shoulder muscles. There came a time in the early fifties when he said that he would never be able to shoot again.

I persuaded him to go to Churchill and adopt Churchill's light-weight 25-inch barrelled guns. Arthur went on to shoot really well to the end of his life; although, at the last, he had to plant his big bottom inside the spare wheel on the bonnet of his Land Rover. From there he put up quite good practice. He reminded me of Lord Rank, who in his last years, got himself lifted into one of those scoops for moving earth so that he could still shoot.

Those memories are nothing in shooting records; but somehow more lasting than the total of big bags. I have vivid memories of shooting in the company of a Norfolk shot named Deterding who, I think, was a member of the banking family. On two-gun days, he would only use a single 16-bore gun. But he had a trick of carrying a third cartridge by the neck between his index and forefinger. He could take two out of a covey of partridges well in front, break his gun, drop in his spare round and take one more behind.

In the manners of shooting, I have no happier recollection than of an occasion when royalty was present. Our distinguished guest was flanked in the line by an elderly member of his household. Whenever a pheasant showed, in which there might have been some doubt as to which gun it belonged to, the man of the court took time off to raise his hat and say, 'Yours, I think, Sir.' If HRH happened to miss, the courtier replaced his hat and killed the bird stone dead behind.

Not all the people I have met in the shooting field have shown manners like that. There were over-eager shots. I remember an odd party in which I was invited to shoot on one of the best moors in Yorkshire. The place had been bought by a rich industrialist. Because he did not know enough guns to invite, he instructed his agent to bring the right people. I was supposed to be one of them.

On the appointed evening, before the two day shoot, we agreed to gather for drinks before dinner in a local hotel. Not many of us knew each other, but we hoped that it would not be long before we did. When we collected, it was noticed that one of the guns was missing. More important, the barmaid was missing too. We couldn't get a drink.

At last, at very long last, the missing gun, and the barmaid reappeared. I often wonder whether it was an accident that the following day on the moors somebody bashed a sizeable dent in the fallible gun's Bentley.

Yet I am entirely on the side, or almost entirely on the side of people who think that there are more important things than knocking down a big bag of game. There was an occasion when I was shooting in North Norfolk, it must have been during the latter part of the war when a large part of the country was being seized for temporary airfields and our host was concerned about bringing in the game which would soon be driven off by concrete runways. With the aid of the armed services, he organised an elaborate system of drives to collect the harvest of birds, and to settle the survivors in more welcome territory. We all shot with two guns, most of us in those days with our wives as loaders; and the drives were as pretty a piece of organisation as Norfolk can show. I seem to remember that they brought the birds over from three different angles.

During the drive, at a stand which should have been the hottest in the line, we noticed crowds of pheasants and coveys of partridges streaming through without a shot being offered to them. The captain of the shot was a North

Norfolk farmer named Frank Case. When he saw what was happening he yelled, 'Whose stand is number seven?'

It turned out that the man who should have been marking it was Henry Williamson who, at that time, was farming in North Norfolk himself. In the explosive inquest after the drive Henry, as indignant as Frank Case, explained that he had put down his gun because he wanted to observe the metamorphosis of a dragonfly in an adjoining ditch.

Neither man could comprehend the attitude of the other. Frank expostulated that Henry had ruined the drive of a lifetime. Henry insisted that he was only there to enjoy himself in his own way. Furious with each other, there was no point of understanding between them. I suppose that I was the only guest present, although I kept very quiet about it, who could see both points of view.

And there was another occasion when I wondered whether huge bags were worth all the trouble. After a stand at the back end of the season when we were shooting cocks only, Lord Iliffe apologised to me that not many birds had shown. 'You can believe it or not, Hastings,' he said, 'but I have seen a thousand dead birds in this field.'

At that moment, Frank Hart the head keeper approached.

'That's right, isn't it, Hart?' asked His Lordship. 'A thousand birds?'

Frank, a veritable Jeeves of a keeper in pepper and salt breeches, carefully oiled boots and carrying a swagger stick like a sergeant-major, confirmed that that was correct. When His Lordship moved on, Frank grinned at me.

'What His Lordship didn't tell you' he said, 'was that it took two lines of us working from dawn to blank in the birds. Then, half way through the drive, we got a message from the guns to stop it. Their weapons were too hot and they wanted to sit down for a rest.'

The memories that I really treasure are those of more modest days, seldom those when we killed a hundred birds to each of our own guns.

The best pheasant I ever shot came at the end of a drive on an experimental farm near Newbury, which was then owned by the magazine *Country Life*. At the end of a drive in which all the beaters were out, and we had unloaded our guns, a cunning old veteran of a pheasant made a last second dash for it. He rocketed straight up into the air, so high that I had time to slip one cartridge back into my gun. The keeper saw me and hollered, 'Twenty to one on the old cock.' With the whole party, guns and beaters looking on, I took him straight over my head, bending back to meet him.

Then occurred an extraordinary phenomenon, something I have never seen before or since. The pheasant pulled up in mid-air, and for seconds – it seemed like minutes – he hung in the air with beating wings. Then he crashed head first and on to his back in the typical tower-bird position of a shot partridge. I mention *where* it happened because someone could so easily read this who was actually there when it happened, shortly after the war. Incidentally, I have always regretted that I didn't take the keeper's bet.

The strangest shot I ever made was at Churchill's old clay shooting grounds at Crayford in Kent. One day I was with his brilliant coach, Norman Clarke who, after Churchill's death, joined Holland and Holland but who is now, alas, dead himself. Surprisingly, a covey of partridges flew over the traps. In fairness, Norman had warned me that it might happen, he knew that the birds were about, but I got a right-and-a-left.

Quite the most uncomfortable shoot I ever attended was at Petworth, when I was a young and inexperienced shot, in the days of the great old Lord Leconfield. 'Lordie' didn't invite me himself. I fancy I was there because another gun had dropped out. As we waited at the first stand, 'Lordie' walked down the line – he had then given up shooting himself – and, addressing each of us in turn said, 'Five hundred pheasants before lunch, sir, or no grace birds for you.' I shot abominably; but fortunately the other guns built up the requisite total. The pheasants were required for the annual tenants' supper.

I think that my most hilarious outing was a day when I was the guest of a very rich man (no names this time) who had reared thousands of birds but couldn't shoot himself 'for toffee'. Because we all wanted to be invited again, the agent who was managing the shoot told a couple of us to see to it that he got a good bag. He announced that there would be no draw for numbers, and arranged that I and another would be on adjoining stands to the great man all day. We poached his pheasants as he let his gun off, warmly congratulating him as we dropped the birds all about him. After that we were invited for the big days every season.

The worst blob I have made was on a flank. A message was shouted up the line from the captain of the shoot at the other end. By the time the message reached me, I had the order 'shoot that cat' as a grimalkin hove into view. I did; to discover that I had shot the best ratter on the place.

It was an illustration of that game they used to play in the army, of passing a word-of-mouth message up a line of men. By the time it reached the far end, the message seldom bore even the vaguest resemblance to the original.

8

THE TYCOONS OF SPORT

The boozy benevolent aristocracy of sport – the world still exists
on the racecourse and in the hunting field – the fabulous Earl of
Lonsdale – Ranji the cricketer – Bendor the Duke of Westminster –
Colonel Peter Hawker and Lord Cowdray – a report on a shoot
attended by the Prince of Wales in Victorian times.

The nineteenth-century nobs in Britain, in the pride of
Empire, were probably the most self-satisfied and amusing
aristocracy that the world has ever known. Because they
had always remained on amiable terms with the tenants on
their country estates, the French Revolution had not
touched them. Master and man played cricket together.
The masters kept the commoners under control by assum-
ing all the higher commands themselves, often disastrously
as it turned out. But from Squire Mytton to the Earl of
Lonsdale, it was all done in a sort of boozy benevolence
which endeared them to their contemporaries.

That they were eccentrics, many of them to the point of
madness, is beside the point. They were larger than life and
people liked them that way. They smoked huge cigars, they
drank pipes of vintage port, they had processions of mistresses and strings of horses and packs of hounds. They
lived in draughty mansions which few of us would be seen
dead in today. They followed field sports in their own
reckless tradition.

It was they who invented 'The Moonlight Steeplechase';
they who thought up 'The Hellfire Club'; they who drove
four-in-hand for fun down to Brighton and up the Bath
Road. It was they who introduced hunting in India,
where there were no foxes, after jackals in the blue
hills of Ootacamund; they who invented driven gameshooting and, in the Highlands, exploited the pursuit of

salmon, grouse and red deer into an expensive and exclusive sport.

It is interesting to observe that the world they created for themselves remains with us, to a certain extent to this day. It still exists, largely on the racecourse and the hunting field; partly in covert shooting, partly on the fashionable salmon and trout streams. I have never thought it a bad thing that it does. On the whole it has encouraged conservation. It has oiled the passing of money from the rich to the not-so-rich; and it has established an intimate relationship, in country life anyway, between all levels in society. But I have never ceased laughing at the excesses of the rich in the past. Nor I suppose did their keepers, huntsmen and grooms.

The classic example is surely the legendary 6th Earl of Lonsdale, the Yellow Earl. Not yellow because he lacked sand, just the opposite; but because he painted all his carriages and farm implements, even his monumental Rolls Royce in that colour. Born immensely rich in the days of the yellow sovereign, he got through a fortune in a long lifetime 'living like a lord'. He was a John Bull of a man, physically very powerful, who adopted side whiskers and wore the square hard hat of the style which was worn by Winston Churchill. His seat was Lowther Castle at Penrith in Cumberland (now Cumbria). He had a mansion in Carlton House Terrace overlooking the Mall. He made himself immortal by his patronage of sport and his grandiose life style.

The hugest Havana cigar is still known by its shape as a 'Lonsdale'. Every day an orchid was despatched to him for his buttonhole, from his hothouses at Lowther Castle. When he went shooting, he took three guns with two loaders. He kept private packs of foxhounds, harriers and beagles. He flew the Royal Navy's white ensign on his private yacht, to the disapproval of the members of the Royal Yacht Squadron, but proved that he was entitled to it by a royal edict awarded to an ancestor appointing him

'Hereditary Admiral of the Coasts of Cumberland and Westmorland and Lord Warden of the West Marches'. When he gave a house party at Lowther Castle, he brought up the ballet company from London to entertain his guests.

To his own people, his arrogance in magnificence must have been appalling. He collected all his keepers with their retrievers together annually for an inspection. If he noted a dog with a grey muzzle he ordered it to be put down. It was a monstrous thing to do because a grizzled dog is almost certainly the wisest dog in the field. But such was the Yellow Earl.

On the other side of the sovereigns, which he cast about with gay abandon, he was the philanthropist, if that's the word, of professional boxing. He awarded the Lonsdale Belt, a dreadful, ornate thing which boxers deck about their bellies, to champions at various weights. In his latter years he became the President of the Bertram Mills Circus at Olympia, making a practice at the opening ceremony of presenting a bouquet to all the circus girls, acrobats, high wire walkers, animal tamers and the rest, and rewarding them with a paternal kiss.

He was the patron of international show jumping long before television made it a popular spectacle. The annual meeting at Olympia was his own show. He provided all the tack painted in his own colour. He presided in his box from beginning to end. Every time a woman rider was announced he left his seat to step down to the floor of the jumping course. As the gates were opened for the girl to enter the competition, he raised his hat in a courtly salute.

I met him in his last years, when after a full life he was almost broke. But Lonsdale in the Mall with a trio of bullterriers walking obediently, so obediently at his heel, was still an impressive figure.

On the eve of the Coronation of George V, he encountered a drunken Cockney in Piccadilly who expressed less than loyal duty to the Crown. Lonsdale knocked him out.

And at the races with King Edward VII, the King said to Lonsdale, as they entered the carriage, 'You first, Lonsdale.' It was quoted to me as an example of perfect manners that Lonsdale never hesitated. If the King wished it, he obeyed. Lonsdale was a nineteenth-century character. I am sure that he gave more pleasure than he took out of life. I would not be writing about him now if I did not feel this.

Politically motivated people of the Left may want to dismiss him and his kind as parasites. But his sort are far more interesting than theirs. What he provided was style, a style which rubbed off into all sections of the country. His money, too.

The attitude of ordinary people to the nobs is summed up, I think, in the classic story of Ranji, the great Indian cricketer. A Cockney invited a friend to join him at the Oval to watch Prince Ranji Singh open the batting for England.

'Now you're going to see something,' he said. 'This is Ranji coming out to bat. Ranji to you and me. But in his own country he's a prince. He rides on a h'elephant before breakfast every morning. He has fountains all over his gardens with houris lining the oriental flower beds for his delectation. He has chests stuffed with jewels, palaces lined with marble, and he has only to flick his little finger and a thousand slaves run to his command. But never mind all that. What you are looking at is the greatest opening batsman in the world. There was never anybody like him, and there never will be. Watch how he takes his late cut. Watch how he lifts a short ball for six. Watch him when . . . Christ, the bloody nigger's out.'

The Indian princes were recognised in Victorian England as 'top drawer'. They joined all the other nobs, even the Lonsdales of the world, in the exercise of expensive field sports. It is told of Ranji that when he bought a salmon fishing river in Ireland – I believe it was Ballynahinch – he gave firm instructions to his keeper that he was not to be disturbed from his carriage until a fish was hooked. The keeper's job was to fish the stream. When he hooked one, he blew a whistle and Ranji came down to land it.

The third Duke of Westminster, another absurdly rich man, did even better. Known to his friends by the nickname of Bend Or – the name of his grandfather's the first Duke's Derby winner – he gave instructions to his head water keeper that he had no interest in coming to the river – the Oikle in the Highlands – unless he could take a fish at first cast. The day came when at last an anxious keeper reported to His Grace that he thought the water was right. The story had a happy ending. The Duke took three fish in three casts.

It is long ago now since the nobs, with their passionate interest in the chase, had it all their own way; the times when the guns were seeded at pheasant and partridge shoots to make sure that the best guns – men like Lord Walsingham, Payne Gallwey and Stonor – had the best stands to ensure big bags. Mercifully the days of big bags for the sake of them are over. I don't know whether they still preserve the covert at Holkham in Norfolk which was only shot when royalty, certain dukes, or Knights of the Garter were present.

There is little arrogance left, the sort of arrogance shown by Colonel Peter Hawker who, shooting in France immediately after the Napoleonic Wars, reported in his diary that he had been plagued by an unruly gundog. He ended: 'At the personal request of Mrs Hawker, I shot the damned dog.'

The modern anecdotes are gentler. It is told that a visitor to Cowdray Park at Midhurst, the seat of Lord Cowdray who is reputedly one of the richest men in England, was surprised to see lines of beaters walking his fields. 'I didn't know they shot on Sundays,' he said. The reply was, 'They don't; but Lord Cowdray has lost sixpence.'

Throughout the story of the nineteenth century tycoons of sport, it is remarkable how little people in the urban centres understood anything about it. Hugh Gladstone, in his little classic *Sporting Records*, reprints a report on a Victorian shoot in the *Liverpool Daily Post*:

THE PRINCE OF WALES AT KNOWSLEY . . . The second full day's shooting at Knowsley yesterday was of a very enjoyable character, and a vast improvement upon the experiences of the previous day. His Royal Highness was early astir, and the glad spectacle of a frost-bound country created the greatest enthusiasm amongst all the sportsmen in the house party. The estate was covered, as far as the eye could reach, with snow and hailstones, a perfect carpet of virgin white being spread out in all directions. Such conditions constitute a sort of elysium for men of the gun . . . His Royal Highness was in excellent health and about ten o'clock in the morning the drags came round to the great entrance. The lordly retinue of the Derbys – gamekeepers, loaders and others – had already proceeded to the objective point of the day, which was at Mosbro, some few miles distant from Knowsley. Only the gentlemen members sallied forth, and they were all in the highest glee, the dry, clear air, the frost and snow, supplying all the zest which the keenest sportsman craves for to whet his enjoyment. The covers over the Mosbro estate, which is an appanage of Knowsley, were in prime condition. Hares were everywhere in abundance, spanking along the fields, or timidly sitting on their haunches, waiting breathlessly for the least sound on the breeze. The rarefied atmosphere acted like a telephonic wire to the wary quarry, and many of them made tracks elsewhere to escape the destructive action of the fowling pieces of the Royal party, as well as the festive pot and prandial accompaniment of appetising jelly. Although every effort was made by the Earl of Derby to preserve the privacy of the Prince's visit, it was found *de facto* absolutely impossible to conceal His Royal Highness's whereabouts. A number of tenants and onlookers from St Helen's and the neighbourhood took up points of vantage, where they could see the sport proceeding, and throughout the day the movements of the Prince were watched with the keenest interest. The house party extended itself in full skirmishing order, and the sport immediately commenced, the pheasants rising in clouds, while the hares spurted out in all directions. The Prince was well to the front all through the forenoon, and the same success followed his fowling piece in the after-part of the day. When luncheon time was called it was felt that the day had proved an ideal one for sport, and His Royal Highness and party sat down in a magnificent marquee on the estate, thoroughly prepared to do justice to the sumptuous fare provided. The tent was fitted up specially for the occasion, adorned with the Royal arms, and the *sans changer* emblem of the ancient house of the Stanleys. After luncheon the sport was resumed and continued with splendid results. His Royal Highness was very successful with his bag, bird and 'puss' falling to his rifle in rapid succession. He overtopped every sportsman on the field in the quantity he brought down. Altogether, over 1,300 head fell to the guns, and the sportsmen, Royal as well as lordly, were intensely satisfied when, fatigued by the arduous duties of their craft – and it is a craft which only the true sportsman knows – they had to abandon the battue, as the dark shades of an early December night began to envelope wood and field, and coppice and bracken, with a pall of impenetrable darkness. It was near six o'clock when the party set off on the homeward journey. Although the ladies at Knowsley took no part in the sport, they evinced the keenest interest in the proceedings of the day, and more than one of them, mounted on bicycles, went to the nearest point where a view of the 'shoot' could be obtained. Such a day's outing was a source of great gratification to all concerned, and the lordly domain of Knowsley bore plentiful evidence in the evening that a unique experience from a field sportsman point of view had been obtained. The Prince seemed fairly well exhausted, in spite of his jubilance, when he alighted from the drag.

9

GAME ON THE HOOK

In Britain you can hang a bird until Easter Sunday – in tropical
countries you must eat game the same day – all game is spoilt by
rough handling – game bags and game pockets are bad – the right
term for birds at the table is 'Harvest of Game' – questions about
wildfowl on the plate – the way to cook pheasants – the still life
painters who hung all their birds the wrong way up.

I used to know a wise old bird who insisted that a javelin-
spurred cock pheasant, shot in late January, would hang
until Easter Sunday whatever the date appointed by the
Pope. In these days of the domestic deep freeze the experiment would be largely irrelevant. Not entirely, because if
you freeze a bird before it is properly matured it will still
come out tough and uninteresting on the table.

In tropical countries there is no question of hanging game
at all; within hours the flesh of bird and beast is rotten. In
Africa and India it is best shot as the sun goes down and
eaten at dinner that night. Surprisingly, in hot countries
game eaten as fresh as that is remarkably tender; as tender, if
not as full-flavoured as a pheasant shot a fortnight before
eating in our own cold climate. I have eaten jungle cock and
jack snipe in India; and guinea-fowl and local species of
partridge on safari in Africa, all within an hour of plucking
them. Perhaps we were just hungry, but they seemed
delicious.

I have never had any doubt that much game is spoilt for
the table by rough handling in the field. On a hot September
day, with all the bluebottles about, hares are particularly
vulnerable. When I was captain of our shoot on the Berkshire Downs, where we shot a lot of hares, I made a rule that
they were carried down to the cellar of a local pub as soon as
a drive was over.

We put our partridges on hand-held racks where they

were slung individually by the neck with plenty of air between them. The racks, I don't know that they are made any more (they were a Victorian notion), had a round-holed end, covered by a brass shutter, to slip in the birds' heads. The necks were then passed through parallel slits in a wooden frame supported by a strong leather strap. The advantage of this device was that you could carry about twenty-four brace without putting a single feather into disarray.

Although I admit that when shooting alone I have perforce used a game bag, even a game pocket, that way of carrying birds is inexcusable from a culinary viewpoint. The birds come out looking as untidy as uncombed hair. They have had no chance to cool. Alas, they are then often condemned to hang in a bunch with other game because there are not enough nails in the outhouse to air each bird equally on its own hook.

In my now long sporting life I have learnt that the ultimate excuse for hunting is the reverence in which the food is brought to table. Early man got a wife by bringing meat into the cave. In the artificial circumstances in which we hunt now, the way in the Western world in which we shoot, the danger for the hunter has gone. It is perhaps a pity. But I recollect a tycoon who, after rearing thousands of pheasants for shooting, was accused of slaughtering them for fun. He remarked, not without logic, 'I gave them life. Surely I can take it away?'

Long ago ICI asked me to look at a film which they had made on their then experimental farm at Fordingbridge in Hampshire, on the rearing of game birds. When I looked at it they had given it some dreary title like 'Shooting Through the Year'. I told them that the title ought to be 'Harvest of Game', which they subsequently adopted. Of course that was the correct title. The conservation of game is no different from the sowing of corn and the reaping of it. No different, although rather healthier, than the system of raising broiler fowls, which appals me although I recognise that it is unavoidable to feed the multitudes in grassless cities.

Sufficient to say that no real countryman would look at one of those broilers spinning on a spit for the satisfaction of poor folk in cities.

In hot temper I have digressed. I wish that I could have answered as well as A. G. Street did when he was asked on 'Any Questions' whether he defended foxhunting. He replied, 'I would no more defend foxhunting than ploughing, sowing, harvesting or any other event in the country calendar.'

I remember an occasion when I was making a film on barley beef, which they run up in less than a year for the urban population. The farmer generously asked the camera crew to lunch. I said that I supposed we were going to have some barley beef. 'Not bloody likely,' he exploded. 'We are going to have a sirloin of four-year-old Aberdeen Angus.'

I am again wandering off the point. Like G. K. Chesterton, in debate with George Bernard Shaw, I can only excuse myself by arguing that 'the art of the duel is to miss the point'.

Back to game and the art of food on the table, which is an endless study. I have been learning it (I have only half learnt it now) since I caught prawns on the rocks in Sussex. An epicure told me in my youth that 'there is no dish on earth, my boy, to compare with the bosom of a plump bird and a bottle of the boy' (partridge and champagne). But truthfully, I have never satisfied myself that there is a golden way of serving wildfowl.

I have enjoyed mallard shot off the inland barley stubbles in autumn, served with an orange sauce. I have loathed eating it when it has been killed in January on the salt marshes. I have never eaten wild goose without wishing I hadn't. As for swan, I was present at a dinner party when a guest threw the roast at his host. The coarse black meat may have been all right for Good Queen Bess; but we have a wider choice of wildfowl now; and the best to eat is surely the teal? For most of the rest, I would be happier to leave them on the wing.

I expect many of you, especially wildfowlers among you, will strongly disagree with me. But would you choose a curlew for dinner in preference to a partridge, a grouse or a pheasant? There is no doubt in my mind that the latter are the gastronomes' choice.

Gamekeepers have given me wise advice. One of them told me never to cook a pheasant in the oven on its back. Lay it on its breast, he said, where the flesh is deepest. He added that the secret is to stuff it with a potato, an apple, or even an onion (if that is your taste) to keep the flesh moist. He did not tell me what I have discovered for myself, that if you stuff a pheasant with English eating chestnuts, you are enriching the meat with the diet which the pheasant eats itself. At one of our local shoots, we used to enlist the girls after lunch to collect chestnuts, and blackberries too, while we were shooting. They made a glorious addition to the later feast.

I know that it is a matter of controversy and taste how long game should be hung. I began this chapter by recording how long an old pheasant might survive without benefit of refrigeration. My own taste is that a September partridge or October pheasant should be hung no longer than a week. According to the weather, I give a November pheasant – pheasants are at their very best when they are stuffed with beechmast or other nuts – about ten days. A December pheasant is normally at its best within a fortnight.

I often wonder how our forebears reckoned it. If you look at still life paintings of the past, you will see that they invariably show game hung by the legs. That is in fact the most hopeless way to hang game, as we all now know. The important thing is to hang it by the neck so that as it matures it drips through the vent. I used to think that the painters were using artistic licence, yet between the seventeenth and the nineteenth centuries they were closer to the land than most people are now. Perhaps our forebears did not find out until later how best to mature flesh for the table.

I have solved many problems of the past, such as why our ancestors held their guns out of balance (they feared, with good reason, that their barrels would blow up). But I still don't know why they hung their game birds by the legs.

10

SHOOTING ABOUT THE WORLD

The best partridge shooting is in Spain – iron barriers defend you
from your neighbouring guns – Spanish pride – the importance of
a secretary – the hare I gave away – the Monteria in the foothills of
Granada – in Mysore in Southern India, a tiger and a rogue
elephant – a lot of old bull – a jungle cock's neck for my flybox –
meeting the wild bushmen of the Kalahari in Central Africa – how
I won their applause – how I won the applause of the Bedouin in
the Jordanian Desert – shooting for the pot in the Canadian Arctic –
how I did not become a prospector.

The best partridge shooting in the world is not at Six Mile
Bottom, Newmarket, but on the meseta about Toledo in
the plains of central Spain. The bag is so predictable that
guns are let by the state on a basis of 500-bird, 1000-bird,
and 1500-bird days. The partridges are all 'Frenchmen'.

To a man who has never shot outside Britain, it is a
bizarre experience to join one of the Spanish shoots. The
guns turn out in cowboy chaps, with tasselled cartridge
bags and hats ornamented with bouquets of fine feathers.
Nearly all of them shoot with over-and-under guns. The
day normally begins with the celebration of Mass in the
open air, joined by the beaters who have begun their own
day with shots of the fiery local brandy at twopence a glass.
Even in December, the sky is likely to be a cloudless blue.

The shoots in the open countryside, which is hedgeless,
are organised with military precision. Mounted men, riding up and down the line, keep the beaters in position. The
guns are posted in stands defended on each side with iron
barriers. The barriers are very necessary, as you can see for
yourself by studying the splashes of shot on them fired by
enthusiastic neighbours. Even so, the sport can scarcely be
called safe. General Franco, none less, lost a finger in the
exercise. I myself had a loader who let off both barrels of
one of my guns behind me within an inch of my heels. But

in Spain, a certain risk is part of the fun. It has something to do with Spanish pride.

A custom, it applies to most of the Continent, is to issue each gun with a card to record what he shoots on each drive. It is an unacceptable custom because, in true sport, there should be no winners. But the way they work it on the mainland of Europe it hardly matters. Each gun has a person who is called 'a secretary', and this secretary is a sort of runner who, after the drive is over, picks up the birds you have shot. The man who shoots the most is inevitably the man whose secretary, at the end of the drive, is the fastest runner, and who can use his fists to the best advantage against the secretary of the man in the next stand. I came to think that part of the charm of the system was just to watch the secretaries exchanging fisticuffs when no shooting was going on at all.

I was surprised when after one drive my loader, who had nearly blown off my legs, asked me if he could have one of my hares. The hares in the meseta of Spain are lighter-framed than ours. As they run down great caverns in the landscape, they provide much more sporting shooting. I suppose that I had shot half-a-dozen of them. I said to the man that of course he could have a hare. He was so conspicuously grateful that I guessed he was thinking that I was doing myself out of a head of game on my wretched card. I was astonished when, on recovering the hare, he hid it under a thorn bush.

After the shoot was over I casually mentioned the matter to a Spanish grandee, another of the guns. Speaking in perfect English, he explained that I had given my man a feast. 'It will be an occasion for the whole family,' he said. 'After the first great meal, they will have a stew. Later, there will be the soup.' Then his lips curled. 'You shouldn't have done it,' he added. I replied to him that that's why the Spanish have civil wars. I think that he did not understand, or did not want to, what I was talking about.

Apart from the hazards of the game, there is no doubt that partridge shooting in Spain is superb. To begin with it is baffling to anybody accustomed to our small-hedged fields, listening for a whistle and knowing that when the covey is over, it is gone. But it is nothing like that in Spain. In the first place, in the meseta about Toledo, you look all about you to a cup which extends to the horizon. The sky is empty of clouds. The sun shines so strongly, that in December, for example, we were picnicking in luxury from a table set out on the plain. To anybody accustomed to English fields, it is at first impossible to judge distance. And worse than that. In the featureless landscape, the coveys driven over the guns swing back and come over the guns again. I was utterly bewildered on the first morning, but in time you get into the rhythm of it. It is certainly a test of any shot. The experience is also enlarged by the slap-happy characters swinging cheerfully across the line and letting off both barrels at the iron barriers – thank God for them – between you.

On another visit to Spain I was a guest at a more formidable exercise. It is called a Monteria. And it was more elaborately ceremonial than the partridge shoots. The preliminary Mass, celebrated under the devout eyes of the hunters, was noisy. The reason was that itinerant masters of hounds, each of them with his own mongrel pack, had closed in from the surrounding countryside. The place was Granada, in the foothills of the Sierra Nevada. The quarry was red deer, roe deer and wild boar. The hounds, each of them equipped with a little brass bell so that his master could identify him in the forest, snarled and barked their way through Mass. The masters – there were about twenty packs – just restrained themselves enough not to knock each other on the nose throughout the sacred proceedings. Then we were off for the hunt.

I felt a sense of alarm when I found myself posted in a butt in which I was totally ringed by caballeros with express rifles. Determining on discretion, I changed my position until I was safely posted behind the trunk of a large tree. Meanwhile, the hounds were loose, creating an appalling noise in the forest below us. I saw a boar, and a deer or two; but could not bring myself to fire a shot. At the end of the day, they brought in boar and stags, and a few various. They also brought in hounds tusked by the boars. I counted myself lucky that I was not included in the various.

It happened in Mysore, in Southern India, where for several days, in the company of a man nicknamed 'Tiger Tim' – he was a senior citizen whose real name was A. C. Thimmiah, and his brother was then Chief of Staff of the Indian Army – we had been on the spoor of a tiger who had got away, and a rogue elephant. Elephants are proscribed by the state as rogues in India when they have killed about fifty people; after that they are anybody's game. If you can catch up with one, it is difficult because they will travel fifty miles in a night, you are entitled to the ivory. Tim and I were out of luck.

True, at first to my great regret, I had shot a rogue bison, the greatest cloven-footed animal in the world. When I raked him, with a double-six-hundred Jeffreys rifle, he went on. After I had followed the blood spoor I found him where he had turned, the brave fellow, to charge me. But he could only lift his head and look at me with his baleful eyes. I felt a complete shit. Although he had been chucked out of the herd, an old bull, I would soon be one myself. Still, it was too late to apologise. The vultures were already gathering.

Then, out of the jungle in which I thought I was quite alone, apart from Tiger Tim and his servants, little men with gaunt bellies and hands held out in supplication appeared out of nowhere. They were villagers who had heard my shot. They had come for the meat for their families. I watched them carve up the carcass, about one and three-quarter tons of it. I saw them in their hundreds trotting home with their little share. I didn't feel so ashamed then that I had killed the old bull. Afterwards, Tiger Tim sent me a trophy of his hooves, made into ashtrays. I hated them. I gave one to a luncheon club I belonged to inscribed: YOU SHOULD HAVE SEEN THE OTHER PARTS OF HIM. They retorted by marking the presentation A LOT OF OLD BULL. They were quite right.

But, on that same shikari, I had a more amusing adventure. I told Tiger Tim that it was my ambition to shoot a jungle cock so that I could use his neck feathers for fishing flies. With typical Indian hospitality he insisted on organising a drive to provide a neck for my flybox. What a drive it was.

People, as they do in India, appeared out of nowhere. We were soon engaged in the loudest drive I have ever been mixed up in. My recollection is that the beaters sounded cymbals and gongs. Tim appointed a man to look after me. My guardian advised me, 'First come peacocks. Don't shoot. They are sacred birds. Next, probably elephants. Run like mad.'

I waited half-hopefully, half-desperately. I saw an animal burst out of the jungle which, at first, I thought might be a leopard. My ghillie, if that's the true word for him, waved his arms excitedly and indicated that I should shoot. I knocked down a huge meercat, and I was told that as a consequence, I was entitled to a state reward of fifty rupees. A few minutes later, there was a disturbance in the palms over my head. I saw a large red animal which I shot. I discovered it was a Malabar squirrel, with a fine for shooting it of fifty rupees. I was all square on the day.

Yes, I got my jungle cock – it was fortunate that there were no elephants about – and I had him for dinner after we had removed his neck. It is illegal – I cannot understand why – to take the feathers of a jungle cock out of India. But I got the skin dressed and smuggled it out in my pocket book.

It is true that most jungle cock feathers on fishing lines are now phoney. The real ones are deadly, especially for sea trout. On a well-dressed fly; the glitter they have cannot be reproduced. I still have a lot to spare for my best friends.

In the arid wastes of the Kalahari in Central Africa, I am fairly sure that a family of wild bushmen still tell the tale of the tall white stranger – in their strange click language they probably sing about it too – who appeared over the horizon of their wilderness bringing them tobacco and salt, and boiled sweets for their children. I found them after trekking for many weeks over a roadless, treacherous terrain in sweltering heat, in which fiery whirlwinds were the main feature of the landscape, and the most important thing was to carry enough water to survive over hundreds of miles of bush and sand. The average speed in our truck, constantly bogged down in anteaters' burrows, was about seven miles an hour.

Optimistically, even foolhardily, I had set out from Bulawayo in search of the last remnant of the aboriginal inhabitants of Central Africa, the bushmen of the Kalahari, the little yellow men whose hair grows in tufts like a pepperbox; nomads following the game with their little bows and poison-tipped arrows, who have never learnt to build themselves anything more than a skerm, an overnight hut. Hunted by white men and black men for generations, they have only survived in a wilderness where other men are still afraid to go.

When they are terrified, and likely to be dangerous, they smile. They conserve their own water in hidden caches of ostrich shells. They can lose themselves in a patch of thorn. The only hope of making an encounter with them is when they are desperately hungry. The family I found were hungry, their bellies drawn up as if they had worms. When they sighted my truck they didn't flee, because they recognised that, if the white man didn't kill them, he had a weapon in his power which brought down meat at great distances. As I drove up to the wizened little men, their stomachs wrinkled like their faces, their slack-breasted womenfolk and frightened children raised their hands in supplication.

I gave them, men and women, cheap black tobacco, which they smoked voraciously through the knuckle bones of antelope. They carried away the rough salt I gave them and hid it in secret places. When I shot a buck with my rifle, they cut it up and simply blackened the meat on a stick over a fire, lighting the fire with a primitive tinder box.

I was astonished by their lack of curiosity. None of the children took the least interest in the tick of my watch. None of the adults was concerned with my battered old truck. They had seen a rifle used before. They seemed, by the way they allowed my companion to photograph them, to recognise that to his particular stranger, they were objects of curiosity. I don't think that they had a clue what the camera was for. They were content – there were about eighteen in the little group – to be fed, and to smoke.

I made, or seemed to make, no impression on them at all, except when towards sundown, when I heard the unmistakable call of a pack of guinea-fowl. Picking up my 12-bore, I followed the birds into thick cover, the bushmen creeping timidly behind me. At last, the guinea-fowl got clumsily into the air. I brought down a brace with a right-and-left. The effect on the bushmen was unbelievable. They collected the birds and, when I got another brace, danced with glee.

It was easy practice. I had taken a much better shot to shoot a springbok for supper with my rifle. I knew that the bushmen could creep up on a sleeping buffalo or a giraffe and put one of their poisoned arrows in its ear. They could then lope after it for miles until the poison worked. But, from their excited gesticulations, I realised that what I had done was outside their own experience. I had picked meat out of the air.

I had gained undeserved fame once before among the Bedouin in the Jordanian desert. On that occasion, I had two Bedouin cameliers and a Jerusalem policeman with a spiked solar topee travelling with me as my bodyguards. Jeeping through the desert, I spotted two sand grouse. I indicated to the swarthy cameliers, with rifles laid across their chests and crossed bandeliers of highly polished bullets, that one of them might care to have a go. He said he had no ammunition, meaning that he had no authority to shoot unnecessarily. I was carrying a little pocket pistol for my own protection. The barrel was no more than three inches, but I aimed in the sand underneath the grouse and, to my own astonishment, lifted one into the air.

When we arrived at the next set of Bedouin tents, for the next round of sheep's milk and mint tea, my cameliers told my hosts all about it. They produced the little bird, and my pistol was solemnly examined by the ring of men squatting in the sand. They were so impressed that they asked if I would do it again. I replied discreetly that I hadn't any more ammunition to spare. But at dinner that night they insisted that I should have the honour of eating the sheep's eye.

In the Far North of Canada, I had a comparable experience. Camping in a blizzard, I had the good luck to shoot a buck when we had nothing left to eat except salt. My companion was a prospector named Wally Brinks. When we got back to the gold settlement of Yellowknife, on the banks of the Great Slave Lake, my pard asked me if I would care to join him in the mineral prospecting game.

'I haven't touched yet,' he said modestly, although he was already running a small aeroplane which landed on the frozen lakes on skids, and had a diamond on one of his fingers as big as the traditional pigeon's egg. 'But I could do with someone like you to shoot for the pot.'

He offered me a generous salary for six months, during

which he would teach me all about prospecting. After that we would go fifty-fifty on every claim he staked. That's how, in a place called Annie's Bar in Yellowknife, eating pork hock, I nearly found a new career for myself.

11

THE COUNTRYSIDE ON TELEVISION

Taking TV into the open air – a lucky trout – a female toad 'shot under protest' – the cock pheasant that wasn't – the mink that was not so tame – how I taught my dog not to chase sheep – the day the technicians forgot to load the film – the hares which couldn't understand poachers' language – the shepherd boy who recognised his sheep – the day I caught a golden eagle – the night when the elvers came up on the Severn bore – the gander who wouldn't face me – the harvest mouse who got lost – the record English carp – Lord Northesk judges dogs – how I was hunted by a pack of bloodhounds – how I faced the steeplechase jumps – riding in Rotten Row with a radio mike – commenting on a rookery – a joke in a country garden.

When I was first invited to appear regularly on TV, in the original 'Tonight' programme, the medium had seldom ventured into the open air. The technicians were highly suspicious, and almost entirely ignorant, of the ways of the countryside. I had to cosset them along.

They jeered when I took them to a spinney where I told them that at twilight the trees would be invaded by a congregation of tens of thousands of migrant starlings. As there was not a starling in sight when we arrived, I had some difficulty in persuading them to set up their cameras. They thought that I was a miracle-maker when, as darkness started to close in, the starlings poured like ink out of the sky. The nasty things – I called them 'Stalins' because they invade us every winter from the Russian steppes – had almost destroyed the wood with their weight and their droppings. The resulting short piece of film created, in its day, quite a sensation.

Soon after this, I took another camera crew to Chew Magna in Somerset, on the first day of lake fishing on the new reservoir. The anglers who lined the banks on the opening day brought in big rainbow trout, which at that time had never been fished, in dozens. But they were all so excited that we could not bring the camera to bear when they played them. The cameraman was contemptuous. So far as he was concerned, they might as well have been fishing for goldfish. I realised that I must try myself to do something about it. With a near mutinous crew, I told them to focus the camera on me as I waded with my rod into the borders of the lake. I told them to roll film, whatever they thought, as soon as I gave them a signal. I won their muttering agreement.

I had the luck of a fat priest. After a cast or two, a trout gave me a tug which indicated his interest. I changed flies and, as my line looped in the air, I signalled 'roll it'. The trout took me exactly when I hoped he would and gave a splendid leap in the air. I played him hazardously so that he gave a good show on the surface. When I had got him at my feet, I gave the crew time to shorten focus before I lifted him into the landing net and offered him in close-up to the lens. It was all done in a single shot of about four hundred feet of film. When the editorial people looked at the sequence in the viewing theatre, they asked me how I had faked it. I began to think that I couldn't win.

It used to be the custom, dating back I think to the old feature film industry, that if a cameraman thought that you were wasting stock he was entitled to mark on his clapper board – the board which is used to chalk up shots in a film – SUP. It means 'Shot Under Protest'. I had to submit to it several times.

There was an occasion when I got hold of a vast female toad – the huge ones are always females – which was almost as big as a dinner plate. She was sitting in bandy-legged satisfaction at the entrance to her hole when I asked the cameraman, once again, to roll it; and not to take his fingers off the trigger until I gave him the word.

I then presented the toad with a magnificent worm. She didn't move, but I saw her brilliant eyes looking it over. For a minute nothing happened except wriggles from the worm. I had to beg the cameraman to keep filming. The climax was everything I had hoped for. At last, at long last, the toad put out a lazy forefoot and pinned the worm to the ground. Then, gathering it up with both feet, she pushed it with ludicrous pantomime down her throat. The long wait in the film, in which nothing happened, created its own suspense. I have often wondered how the cameraman explained that clapperboard, marked SUP, which prefaced the sequence before it was edited.

Not that my own face was never red. I remember a time when I was making a short film on a pheasant shoot in Suffolk. It is always terribly difficult to line up cameras, which are obstinately heavy things, with the man handling the gun and, more unpredictably, the flight line of the birds. It was a cocks-only day, and nothing came right to bring the three factors of camera, gun and bird together.

At desperate last, I suggested to my host that with his permission we might settle for a hen if she flew on the line we wanted. We got excellent shots of tall birds being pulled down; and I took care that what the dogs picked up in the film were cocks. But I was sufficiently worried to ask to see the film on the big screen in the viewing theatre. I satisfied myself that on the small screen, on a sequence made on a winter's afternoon, no one would know whether the birds that were dropped were cocks or hens. I had two letters – just two, but enough – reminding me that I had in fact said that day, it was 'cocks only'.

Another time I was ticked off in letters from three very well-known game shots for lifting the barrels of my gun to the butt, instead of raising the butt to the barrels as I loaded. They were, of course, quite right. But they had never faced the problem of handling a gun so that the lock plates would not make a flash in the lens of the camera; and the gun, as it was loaded, would not be out of focus.

But the best joke on me was when I 'interviewed' what

was described as a tame mink. Mink are normally unman-
ageable, but I was introduced to one who was making itself
at home in somebody's sitting-room. To demonstrate how
friendly it was, I undertook to lift it out of its box. David
Attenborough still won't let me forget that when I put my
hand in, the evil fitch locked into it. When I pulled my hand
out, with the mink still attached, I shouted to the camera
crew 'cut'. They didn't need a second warning. Blood was
spurting out all over the place.

We managed to get a second shot in which the mink
behaved as a 'tame' mink should. But, very properly, the
'Tonight' boys decided to use the first, in which I shouted in
anguish 'Cut'.

I was in the Lake District when, on the spur of a moment in
which another story had folded and I was reminded how
much it cost the BBC to keep a unit in the field doing
nothing, I decided that it was an appropriate time to teach
the dog I had then not to chase sheep.

I had named him Friday (no relation to James Robertson
Justice's dog), because he had shared with me a sojourn on a
desert island in the Indian Ocean. I am sorry, but that story
is not for now. It must suffice that Friday, who was a sort of
cross between a bull terrier and a dachshund, was an ideal
companion for a Robinson Crusoe. After a six months
quarantine, he was unable to distinguish between land crabs
and hill sheep; he attacked the lot. It was necessary, and I
believed that it might instruct the huge TV audience, that I
should give him a sharp lesson.

As usual I had to persuade the film technicians, from the
pale and artificial world of London studios, that I knew
what I was up to. I had no script to give them. I had to talk
'off the cuff', as they say in the trade.

I persuaded a farmer, with a flock of empty ewes who
were unlikely to come to any harm, to let me turn Friday in
among them. When the cameras were ready, I set Friday

loose. He had a whale of a time tumbling and somersaulting the sheep all over the field. I began my commentary with the words: 'I am sorry to tell you but that's my dog.'

I then applied the treatment widely employed in Lakeland to teach Fell Hounds their proper business. We put Friday in with an old well-horned ram in an enclosure of hurdles. The ram butted him until his muscles ached. I then took him into the field where the ewes were.

'Go on, Friday,' I said, 'chase sheep.'

He averted his head, and after that you could not believe that he had ever noticed a sheep in a field. The treatment lasted, at most, not more than ten minutes. The punishment that Friday tasted could be reckoned, in human terms, not more than three rounds to the loser in a boxing bout.

The programme, when it went on the air, lasted not much longer than *one* round of a fight; and the response from the audience was incredible. Letters came by the sackful, far too many for the usually efficient BBC correspondence department to deal with. The mail broke into three categories. The first were people who said that I ought to be prosecuted for cruelty; the second, from farmers praising me for showing how to control an unruly dog; and the third, far the greatest, from people who wanted me to introduce them to a ram who would teach their animal that he must not chase sheep. Surprisingly, I still get letters today, years later, about those few minutes on the air.

Friday, alas, has now gone to the happy Hunting Grounds, where I suspect he also still tells the story.

I have had dreadful luck with cameras nearly as often as I have tasted success. In the same way, I suppose, the birds in the shooting field you inexplicably missed, and the fish that got away, they make a more indelible impression than the moments when everything goes right.

I have lasting memories of a morning when we were filming the metamorphosis of a mayfly. It was a difficult subject but I felt we had brought it to picture, only to discover that the experts had forgotten to load film into the camera. Another time we made a difficult landing on a sand bank off the east coast to photograph the seals. We had to hump the cameras on our backs in treacherous waist-deep water, under the direction of the coxswain of the local lifeboat. When we had made it, we discovered that the studios had forgotten to load any of the film magazines.

But it is not fair to blame everything that went wrong on other people. I must be held responsible for misjudgements too. In North Norfolk I had met 'Kenzie', the more or less reformed poacher, about whom Colin Willock has written a book. Kenzie demonstrated to me how he could call a hare across the field to his feet by pursing his lips and emitting a sort of squeal. In Norfolk it worked.

I brought Kenzie to Hampshire, to Lord Rank's estate at Sutton Scotney. When he called to the Hampshire hares, they did not as much as flick an ear. Apparently he had the wrong regional accent. We tried again later in Norfolk and the hares all answered his call as if he were Francis of Assisi. We made a remarkable film up there.

I learnt a lot of things under the extra discipline of the cameras. For example you read a lot in angling textbooks about the need to strike or, more properly, tighten on a rising fish. It happened that I wanted to make a sequence of a trout taking a fly. Because I faced the problem of the fish having to take the fly within focus of the camera, I asked Alfred Lunn, the great head keeper of the Houghton Club at Stockbridge, whether I could stage the shot in one of his crowded fish stews, where the fish rose to anything. Cutting the barb off the hook, I cast the fly for the camera. It was taken again and again. The remarkable fact is that, when the fish rose and carried the fly to the bottom, I had to pull the barbless shank out of their mouths. So much for the importance of timing the strike.

I have never in fact believed that the strike matters much. One day at Testwood in Hampshire, which is arguably the very best salmon pool in Britain – yes, Britain – I was floating a line to help the cameraman make his set-up on me. I picked on a little whirlpool which hung my fly in a fixed position. I waited while the unit moved the camera about, settled the tripod, fixed me up for sound. At last, everything was ready.

My fly must have been floating about in the little whirlpool for minutes. They clapped the board for the first shot. At the precise moment, a salmon took me. He must have been watching my fly all the time. The moral, of course, is that you cannot fish salmon too slow.

Latterly, the 'Tonight' office showed a touching faith in my ability to produce what to them, in Lime Grove, seemed inconceivable. A day came when they told me of a case reported in a provincial paper in which a shepherd boy in Wales, appearing as witness in a sheep-stealing case, said simply that he knew the ewes were stolen because he recognised them. Could I find someone, they said, who could recognise sheep?

I discovered a farmer in the West Country whose flock were, I seem to remember, about five hundred pedigree Dorset Horns; the farmer told me that he could identify every sheep in his flock. His performance staggered me, and I wish I could remember his name.

When the flock had been rounded in, I stood in the milling mass of wool with a microphone attached to about fifty yards of cable. The farmer stood back beside the camera. Whenever I indicated an animal, he gave me the correct number of the tag on its ear; and, for good measure, told me its lambing history as well. I have never seen a more brilliant demonstration of the craft of husbandry. The boy in Wales was right. A good shepherd can recognise every individual in his flock.

What I thought was going to turn out to be one of my failures, turned out to be my luckiest break. I was in Lewis in the Hebrides when I heard of a golden eagle's eyrie which, the stalker said, was sufficiently accessible to hump the camera to it. It was a heavy trudge and a heavy climb but, together with the crew, we managed it. And, to our delight, there was a single bird, almost fully grown, in the nest. I reckoned that it was the female, and that if there had been a second bird she had tumbled it overboard. It often happens.

We had no difficulty in lining up a splendid shot, although the adult birds were then pinpoints over the sea. The camera rolled, but we were at once in trouble. The high whine of a camera mechanism has an extraordinary effect on wild animals. Horses, dogs, and other domestic animals will cock their ears with interest; but again and again it sends wild animals into a panic.

The eyas in the nest was no exception. With a flurry of wings, she took off from her nest on the cliff. She was obviously making the first flight of her life, flying as clumsily as a novice pilot on a 'circuit and bump'. She crashed on the beach at the base of the cliff and it was plain that she wouldn't take off again. Like a mountain sheep, the tough Highland stalker went after her. Within twenty minutes he brought her back in his arms.

The light was failing. The camera crew reckoned that they had little more than fifteen minutes of filming time left. I laid the huge bird on my lap, her great yellow talons stretched out in front of her, her wings spread to the full reach of my arms. With her great eyes, fixed on me, like pools in a burn, I talked about eagles. It was quite an experience.

Years later, a golden eagle escaped from the London Zoo. Nobody could catch it. Unduly flattering me, the BBC repeated my programme, adding that the Zoo ought to send for me. But I could never have done it twice.

Early on in the 'Tonight' programme, I thought I'd find out whether the Severn Bore, the great tidal wave which, in its

season, can reverse the flow of the river as high as Tewkes-
bury Lock (some thirteen miles above Gloucester) had ever
been filmed. I was surprised to learn that it never had been.
It started me off on quite an adventure.

The appearance of the wave, in obedience to lunar laws,
can be calculated to the second. The problem was to film it
sweeping up a big river on a dark night. The BBC agreed
that we should need two cameras, one to catch the wave as it
approached, the other to screen it receding. As it was going
to happen at night, we rigged a chain of powerful flares to
illuminate the scene during the vital moments when the
Bore swarmed up the river. It worked like a charm. At the
exciting zero hour, we flooded the Severn with light. We
got our film of the great race of water. But what nobody
had told me was that there were scores of others, sitting
patiently on both banks in the glimmering light of lanterns,
waiting as we were for the appearance of the Bore. We had
totally blinded them with our own display of light. When
our flares died and the air was sizzling with four-letter
words, I was to discover that we had pinched their fishing.

It is a phenomenon that in its wave the Severn Bore
carries millions, surely billions of elvers back from the sea
into freshwater. The men with their lanterns were there to
scoop them out. The eels, little translucent things, about
two or three inches long at that stage of their growth, are
attracted by light. I had thrown so much light that they
were all under my bank. In a net I scooped them out by the
bucketful and, by way of an apology, gave them away to
the chaps on the bank. They, in turn, sold them quickly to
salesmen who had arrived from the Low Countries and
Germany, who wanted to release them in their own rivers.
The fishermen also sold them, at good prices, to people
who wanted the baby eels for the North Country and
Spain, where they are counted a delicacy. I have since eaten
them in Madrid and, for my part, you can keep them.

Odd experiences became an everyday part of my work. If

the story wasn't odd, it wasn't worth telling. I remember failing hopelessly when I advertised in *Country Fair*, which I was then editing, for a gander who would see anybody off. I got a lot of replies from people who claimed that their own goose would beat up anybody who came into his yard, and I picked on one who had the reputation of dealing with the postman, the milkman, the grocer and the newspaper boy.

I arrived with the BBC crew to give the viewers the fun of letting the gander see me off, too. He sallied forth, with his wives in attendance, his wings set for trouble. I told him to 'have a go'. He considered me for a moment out of his blue eyes and then, to my vast disappointment, turned tail. The trouble was that he knew that I wasn't frightened of him. Worse, I was laughing.

After the goose, I had a calamitous experience with a harvest mouse, the smallest mammal in the British Isles. Harvest mice, once so common, are now relatively rare. They are victims of modern methods of corn cultivation. But I heard of a pair in the children's section of the Natural History Museum in South Kensington. It was agreed to bring them down to my cottage in Berkshire, and to make a film of them doing their acrobatics among the wheat stalks.

We built an artificial box of wheat in one of the bedrooms, where we were sure they couldn't get away. In close-up, we got a wonderful film of them showing people like Olga Korbut how to do it. When we had finished, we realised that one mouse was missing. We failed to find a hole where he could have got out. The naturalist who had brought him from the museum put the other one in a jam jar, and returned disconsolately to London.

The following morning, as I was writing, I seem to remember, an urgent obituary for *The Times*, I saw the missing mouse running over the floor. Somehow he had got downstairs. I capped him with another jam jar. But I couldn't carry him back to London because I had an appointment at the Royal Agricultural Show, so I took him with me in a biscuit tin.

Finally, I returned him to the Natural History Museum where he survived with his mate for a year or so (remarkable because, in the wild, the life of a harvest mouse is a mere month or two). At the Royal Show, I venture to think that he attracted as much attention as the pedigree animals. Countrymen, hearing what I had got, all crowded round to look at him.

I had no part in the adventure when Richard Walker of Hitchin caught his record English carp; although I subsequently made a film for BBC about the great fellow in the aquarium of the London Zoo. I am sorry to record that the biggest carp ever taken out of British waters – forty-four pounds of him – has at last died.

The story of Dick Walker's catch is the more remarkable because he forecast that he would do it. Until he hooked the monster in the early hours of the morning in a lake in the West Country, the biggest common carp in the British Isles was thought not to exceed much over twenty pounds. Dick thought differently. He insisted that carp of up to fifty pounds and more, were flourishing in our waters. He was so certain of it, the angling boffin that he is, that he prepared to prove himself right by designing his own Mark IV Carp Rod to fish it. He has shown me the mathematical formula on which he based the rod. It was as bewildering to me as the specifications of Concorde. Not content with that, he also constructed a vast landing net, calculated to lift anything up to ninety pounds in weight out of the water. Only then did he lay siege to the monster, which only *he* believed existed. It is angling history that he caught the great fish at exactly 4.45am, and brought it to his net in ten minutes on 13th September 1952.

When the battle was over, and the fish was encompassed in his landing net, Dick recognised that he had another problem. He couldn't put it back into the water because nobody would believe that he had caught it. And he didn't care to knock it on the head and put it in a glass case. But he had the brilliant notion of calling up the aquarium at the London Zoo, and asking them if they wanted it. To the Zoo's great credit, they sent out a van with a tank aboard to collect it.

Ravioli, as he was called, lost weight in his latter years. But I remember him gulping slices of bread from my hand in his toothless mouth. He confirmed the reputation of an angler; and he had a happy ending.

I have the happiest memories of a day at the Cheltenham Ladies Dog Show when I asked Lord Northesk, then Vice Chairman of the Kennel Club, whether I might film him judging a class. He looked himself like an elderly dog and, as a judge, he had an inimitable show ring style of his own. He performed a sort of dance, with a flurry of gestures, as he assessed the dogs. I told him in advance that I intended to film him as he worked, without any commentary from me. He saw the joke and played up to it.

We put out the film, to the music of 'The Nutcracker Suite', in which Northesk never put a heavy foot wrong. I thought he might be furious. But the dear man, whose hobbies were gundogs, model railways and fast cars, was delighted. All he wanted, and he got it, was a copy of the film. (Incidentally, Northesk took all the speedometers out of his Bentleys. He said that he knew when he had passed seventy miles an hour because his Labradors withdrew their heads from the open windows.)

My adventures with dogs included a day when I was hunted by a pack of bloodhounds, mastered by a dentist from Chesterfield in the Derbyshire Peaks. On that day I was the quarry. It is, of course, a fallacy that bloodhounds are fierce creatures. In kennels you certainly need to be careful with them, but in the field they are so delighted to run you to ground that all they try to do is to lick you into it.

On that exploit in Derbyshire, I learnt two interesting facts. The hardest test you can give a bloodhound is to ask him to separate the trails of identical twins. It is also true, if you happen to be in conflict with the law, that the hardest trail for a bloodhound to follow is a man in gumboots. Leather boots leave a knee-high scent. Rubber is deceptive.

With the BBC film cameras I was sometimes tempted to experiment too much, like the day when I rode with Dick Francis, none other, over the steeplechasing jumps on Frank Cundell's gallops on the Berkshire Downs. I was riding an old chaser named Crudwell, who had already won forty-nine races. The idea was that the film would be transmitted when he won his fiftieth, as he did.

The cameraman, as demanding as ever, made me jump again and again, close-ups of the horse taking off and landing-down, a distance with a good steeplechaser of perhaps thirty feet. After half-a-dozen attempts, I realised that I was then fifty years of age. It was only all right if I stayed in the plate. I swore to God I would never do it again; and I never have.

I had an even worse experience in Rotten Row in Hyde Park, of all places. It was in the days when the BBC was experimenting with radio-microphones. The notion was that I would broadcast a commentary while I hand-cantered a horse along the Row. The microphone was strapped to my saddle. We pulled it off, the horse and I both lathering with the strain of keeping level with the camera running beside us on 'a dolly', and with me trying to remember what to say. They do it better now.

Time and again, I have been a guinea-pig. I am not likely to forget the occasion when I was asked to make a commentary on a rookery filmed on a high rise camera in the West country. I couldn't see what the camera saw looking down over the trees. All I had was a monitor which wasn't working properly. I had to throw myself flat on my back in the grass to make a guess at what was going on. And I was later told that my own insufficiency had made the programme a success. I wouldn't suffer it again.

I think the happiest idea I ever had was at a time when the garden in my Berkshire cottage was in an awful state. It was in the years, shortly after the war, when small horticultural machinery was just coming on the market. I made contact with all the new manufacturers and told them that they could bring everything they had got to put my garden in order. To see their machines demonstrated on TV suited them fine.

So it happened. I had myself filmed digging in the wilderness of the garden, as it was. Then, with the magic of Snow White and the Seven Dwarfs, I opened the garden gate. In poured a chain of men with every machine then available on the market. In a few hours, the hedges were trimmed, the lawns were cut, the garden was dug, the roses were pruned, and the whole place was made as tidy as a clean well-folded handkerchief.

At the end of the film, I went back to showing myself working in an untended garden, dreaming of the sort of miracle which I had just showed happening. The BBC got a lot of letters from viewers, telling them how sorry they were that my garden couldn't be tidied up as I had hoped.

12

ADVENTURES IN SEA FISHING

The big tunny who weren't there – the whale who was – the sharks
who obliged and the camera crew which didn't – the appetite of a
herring gull – the handline fishermen of Malabar – the sea snakes of
the Indian Ocean – the Sacrifice Islands – fighting the stingrays –
comparing fishing in tropical seas with northern rivers – the ever-
lasting lugworm.

Fishing for me has never been Isaak Walton's *Contemplative Man's Recreation*. My recollections largely consist of the times when I have tumbled into the water, lost my gear, or encountered some monster of the deep who got the better of me.

In sea fishing, although I have caught my share, I have been singularly unfortunate. Just for a start, I remember the time when enormous tunny were being caught off Scarborough. (They have gone away now.) Optimistically, I put out in a Brixham trawler to go after them. The pattern of the exercise was to join the boats ring-netting the herring. The big tunny, like the fishermen, followed the shoals.

In the pale light of dawn, we put out a rowboat from our trawler into the fleet of herring-fishers. I harnessed myself to the big game tackle in the stern in preparation for a fight with a big fish. The netters who hailed us had sighted no tunny at all. They could only comfort us by letting down baskets of herrings for our breakfast. I grew increasingly gloomy. Then, as we paddled along in the little rowboat, I saw a real big 'un. He swished past us with a quiet sweep of his tail.

On one of the herring boats a look-out shouted to us to take care. It was a whale, he called. Not very big as whales go; but probably about a ton. Next, within feet of us, he blew a spout. It smelt like all the bad fish in a lifetime. We rowed until our muscles ached to the safety of our Brixham

THE ONE THAT GOT AWAY: Fishermen seldom provide a picture of their failures. Fellow guests on the bank of a Highland stream hold an inquest on one of mine. The ghillie looks on aloofly.   (see *The Hazards of Fishing*)

SOME WHO DIDN'T: On the big days in the flat lands of East Anglia, a guest who misses too often is unlikely to be invited again. Here are the sort of shots who fire ten thousand rounds in a season.   (see *Great Shots*)

HENRY WILLIAMSON, the author, on his Norfolk farm out shooting with the author. Note the period style of the cloth caps.

JAMES ROBERTSON JUSTICE, the actor, bringing one of his peregrine falcons to the lure. Grouse-hawking in Inverness-shire.

SPORTSMEN THEY

MICHAEL JOSEPH, the author's publisher, during a successful day's fishing at Testwood in Hampshire. Terry, with the fish, is the famous keeper on the beat.

A. G. STREET, the celebrated farmer writer, with the author at a convivial house party.
(see *Our Comic Opera Shoot, Odd Birds, et alia*)

THE FOG OF BLACK POWDER: This is what the old gunners in the early nineteenth-century sporting prints had to contend with. They could only shoot at going-away game with a raking shot because flint guns had a time-lag of a fifth of a second between trigger pull and fire. The smoke from the change subsequently obscured vision of the quarry. (see *Shooting with a Muzzleloader*)

trawler. A flick of his tail would have sunk us. I never had a chance at a big tunny again.

I am unlikely ever to forget the basket of herring which his ring-netters lowered into our boat. When I came aboard our trawler, as hungry as any hunter, I asked our skipper to grill some of them for breakfast. Just after dawn, the sun was still only a pale orb in the sky. 'If we cook them now,' he said, 'so soon after taking them out of the nets, they'll blow up. They need a couple of hours sunshine on the deck to mature.' To prove his point, he squashed one of the largest herring in the palms of his hands. He worked it round in his grasp until, like a conjuring trick, the herring disappeared. All that was left was a coat of oil. Herrings have no solidity in their flesh until they have been out of their own element for a few hours.

After failing with tunny, I had better luck with sharks; but that luck had its hazards. I put out from Looe in Corn-wall in the hopes that I might join the company of fisher-men with fish sizeable enough to join the Shark Club. A television camera crew were with me, who laboured under the delusion that with a ration of seasick pills, they would be quite safe. We had scarcely passed the harbour mouth when the lot of them were flat on the deck in hopeless sea-sickness.

Eight miles from land, when we were flapping rubby-dubby (pilchard oil) on the side of the boat to attract the mackerel and after them the sharks, I had a crew who, apart from the fishermen, were completely out. I remembered a time in the war when I was aboard a motor launch, escort-ing a convoy up the Channel. It was rough weather and the whole crew collapsed with seasickness, including the cap-tain. When at last the Commodore of the convoy told us to go home – as a fighting force we were negligible – it was left to me, with a captain on his back instructing me, to guide us into Poole Harbour. It happened on the shark-fishing expedition all over again. But it was a success as such things go. I caught the sharks, although not the big ones which we hoped for. What I had to contend with, never mind the fish, were people lying on their backs in the bilge, saying 'Oh God, he's caught another one!' I brought home seven, but I came home without any feeling of success.

When we got into the harbour again, with a load of mackerel, I remarked on a herring gull sitting on the bow. 'He wants a mackerel,' the fisherman said. I threw him one which the gull shook down his neck. 'He can eat more than that.' I threw him a second, a third and a fourth. 'He can't take off after four mackerel,' I said. 'He will.' And indeed he flew away as if he had eaten nothing at all.

I have always been a bad fisherman. I could never equal those men in the Indian Ocean, off the Malabar Coast, who using only handlines could land those huge mackerel, seer, sailfish and the rest, up to two hundred pounds, without scoring their fingers. They just sat there, in their little boats under vast straw hats, playing fish that would extend any Western angler with the best tackle he could buy. I have never seen men fishing handlines with such skill; and I am inclined to think that the Malayalees (Rain People) are the finest anglers in the world. They don't use a frame for their lines. They cast from the coil and play their fish with their fingers. That they are constantly able to cast a long coil of line from the hand and gather it again without ever making a bird's nest, is clever enough. But to play a fighting fish of forty . . . fifty . . . even a hundred pounds on a handline is a breathtaking thing to do. If you or I tried to hold a line with a fish that size at the other end, he would either break us immediately or tear the line through our hands so fast that it would burn off our fingers.

Half-naked men, with skins the colour of old pennies, can run out line, disputing it back again with no more than a dance of control. They never lose a fish. Sometimes, when they bring them in to the hollowed tree trunks they use as boats, the fish is half the size of the craft. But, giving him a quick knock on the nose with a club, they always have him.

I fished with the natives on shore again and again. I pulled their seine nets with them when they drew in. There were always sea snakes in the purse. They are remarkable creatures, which you can watch in the Indian Ocean throwing their tails in the air as they sink underwater. I am told that they are the most poisonous snakes on earth. But there is no record that anyone has been bitten by one. When the seines were drawn in, the children threw the sea snakes back into the water.

Fishing in the Indian Ocean, it did not seem important what I caught. Huge fish, coloured in the spectrum of the rainbow, littered the deck. It was the heat that mattered. At noonday we sheltered in the Sacrifice Islands. They were called the Sacrifice Islands because at the beginning of every season a few hundred years ago, a virgin was slain on the altar to ensure good fishing in the next year. In my day, I sheltered in the Islands from the heat to pick oysters out of the shallows and shoot doves who dived out of the caves in the rocks.

I have had reasonable luck fishing in the North Sea and the English Channel, the best days bringing back a load of tope, plaice and flounders, when we had the good fortune to drop anchor on an old wreck. I have caught flounders with a trident on the Solway Firth. And I have had to hunt fish for a living on a desert island.

I threw myself away deliberately on a desert island about sixteen years ago to discover how I would survive on the Boy Scout's traditional knife and a piece of string. I chose an island in the Indian Ocean, and I have written about the adventure elsewhere.★ All that matters here is the fishing. My main diet was the stingrays which have tails like hunting whips and a poison spine in the middle. I killed them with a sharpened stake. They fought formidably; but when

★*After You, Robinson Crusoe.*

you are hungry you can fight back. I wouldn't recommend stingrays, a form of huge skate which cruise on the surface of tropical lagoons, their eyes like submarines with their periscopes up, as a regular diet. I had made sea salt in my isolation to make them more tolerable. But subsequently, the dieticians told me that I had made a mistake in cooking them. If I had eaten them raw, I would have digested more valuable vitamins. My dog Friday, who I had taken with me, knew better than I did. He kept on stealing the great steaks of raw fish when I filleted them. He came off the island, when they rescued us, in top order – which was more than I did.

True, I have had splendid fun sea fishing in most of the oceans of the world; sometimes in acute discomfort, often in the luxury of yachts where you only had to raise your hand for someone to place an iced drink in it. But sea fishing has never for me had the thrill of fishing wild northern rivers for salmon and trout. It is the fastidiousness of fishing freshwater which is so fulfilling.

In sea fishing the salt makes your tackle sticky, your hands inevitably become cold and rough. I have taken huge cod in Norway when all you needed was a bare hook loaded with lead. The sea bed was so thick with fish that if you had a strong pull, you inevitably foul-hooked. After a session in a little boat I was always glad to go home.

All right, I know that there is an art in fine fishing in the sea. I have spoilt a trout rod searching for mackerel on the west coast of Britain. The trouble is that a hooked mackerel won't fight you on the face of the water. He immediately submarines. The only sea fish which fight in the waves, apart from the tropical ones, are those salmon of the sea, the bass. But I hate it when I bring back fine tackle from the salt. My own delight is the beauty of the action of a rod, a high precision reel and a streak of line caressed by a run of water in fresh streams.

I go along with a friend of mine who told me that he went

sea fishing seriously only once. He was advised that he needed some lugworms for bait. When he threaded a lugworm on his hook, it bit him. When he lifted his bait, long after, there was only three-quarters of an inch of lugworm left. It bit him again.

13

NO TALL STORIES

Fishermen's tales – some true ones – the fish I had in a flood on the
Aberdeenshire Dee – the hook that I fished with a broken barb –
and the man who mended it.

In my first novel* I described the capture of the most
notable salmon of the 1949 season, a cock fish weighing
fifty-seven pounds three ounces, and taken on a No. 7
Hardy's L.W. Blue Charm. I called the stream in which the
fish was killed the Edendale, a thinly-disguised union between the upper waters of the Helmsdale and the estuary of
the Naver in Sutherland. It must have been a convincing bit
of fiction, because ever since I have been asked whether it is
correct that I have ever caught a salmon by fair fishing of
over fifty pounds.

Ten years later, I wrote another novel† in which I
indulged myself in a fancy that it was on a night that Big
Ben tolled disaster by striking twenty times at three o'clock
in the morning, that the last of the vanished race of Thames
salmon ran up the river. As a result of that piece of fiction, I
have seen recorded in the correspondence columns of *The
Field*, none less, that I have asserted that the last Thames
salmon came up on the tide of 21st March 1861.

Thus are fishermen's tales born.

Writing as one who can truthfully say that he has caught
two trout with one fly, and has recovered a prawn tackle
from a fish which broke him, I don't want to be on record as
one of the liars. The second trout, going for the fly after the
first had had it, tied the gut into a grannie knot under his
gills. The salmon I lost struck me, after I had consoled
myself with a half bottle of claret, on the first spin after

* *Cork on the Water.*
† *A Glimpse of Arcadia.*

lunch. It happened on that prolific salmon pool Testwood, at Totton in Hampshire. With four tides running up and down the Solent, fresh run fish come up the estuary of the Test twice a day.

I have had many adventures there with many friends. One autumn evening, I was fishing with Michael Joseph, then my book publisher, when there was a remarkable run of sea trout, none of them weighing less than three and a half pounds. We lost one, at the last unforgiving moment, before scooping him into the landing net which Terry, the water keeper, estimated was all of eighteen pounds. I didn't know it but Michael was then on his last legs with a duodenal ulcer. He could not carry on until dusk although Terry told us we could expect that day to hook fifty trout. When we stopped we had about ten.

While I cannot think of any pool, even in Scotland, which yields the quantity of fish that Testwood does, it is important to add that it is lawn-fishing. Angling there has nothing of the rugged excitement of the northern rivers.

The most memorable fish I ever killed in my life was on the Aberdeenshire Dee when it was in frightening flood; such a flood that whole trees and drowned hill sheep by the dozen were carried down in the current. Wading would have been impossible. My ghillie, the most taciturn of Highlanders, announced, 'You'll noo catch a fush this day.' To emphasise his point, he retired sulking with his pipe to the fishing hut.

But I was only up on Deeside for a week, and I was determined to have a go. I selected the biggest fly I had in my box, a 'Thunder and Lightning', about three inches long. I put up an old Grant's Vibration greenheart rod I had – I still have it – and spliced the joints together with camera tape. Balanced gingerly on the bank, I cast into the cataract which was running, as Chesterton wrote in *Old Noah*, 'as if it would wash the stars away as suds go down the sink'.

I had made no more than half-a-dozen casts, stretching

the distances with a 16-foot rod, squaring my legs to keep my balance as the current took the big fly into its embrace, when I felt the delicious double-tug of a big salmon. With the current on his side, he gave me no pause to reflect on the situation. He ran me out to the backing straight across the raging Dee. I fought him, most of the time, on what I thought must have been seventy yards of line. Only the length of the rod enabled me to avoid getting snagged in the debris which was swirling down the river.

I concentrated as best I could on keeping below him. But with every step downstream I was drawing nearer to a row of withies, or whatever they were on the bank. With the butt of the rod pressed to my belly, I gave the fish all I knew to throw him off balance. At last he began to swing in a long arc. I gained line. How long I played him, I don't know. It must have been twenty minutes, with the formidable current of water on his side, and when at last I got him to my bank I still hadn't won.

There was a fall of about six feet to the level of the water. Fortunately I had a telescope gaffe. But I had to play him out completely before, holding my heavy old rod in one hand, I lay on my face and reached, just reached far enough, to lift him out of the water. He weighed twenty pounds.

I had no sooner grassed him than I was rejoined by my reluctant ghillie. Even the dour Highlander could not conceal his astonishment. I remarked to him – it is an old principle of salmon fishing – that the brother of my fish would be waiting for me. I worked up a long cast to reach into the deep water where I had caught the first.

Sure enough, another big fish took me almost on the surface as the fly hit it. I had him on for a few seconds – and then he was gone. Disconsolately, I reeled in to discover that in my excitement I had hit a stone on the back cast. It had fractured the barb off the hook.

For years I kept that 'Thunder and Lightning' in my fly book just to remind me never to let such a silly thing happen again. Then, one day, I lent my collection of flies to a fishing friend. When he returned the book he sent a note with it to say that he had noticed a fly with a broken shank. He had re-tied it as a way of saying thank you.

14

THE HAZARDS OF FISHING

The American Ambassador who lost an eye – the man who tried to stop a fresh run salmon running downstream – fishing in deep water for a salmon in the shallows – losing my feet with a fish on in the Aberdeenshire Dee – the angler who was hooked by a fellow fisher – the man who caught his fly in the lobe of his ear – the five pound bet I won promising to hook a fish – the bottle of champagne I won hooking a blind one – the fishing story which ended happily ever after.

The great old music hall comic, George Robey, used to tell the story of a friend of his named Tallulah Treeherd, who had only one ear. 'She lost the other pike-fishing.'

Like so many jokes, there is an element of bitter truth in it. The American Ambassador, Lewis Douglas, casting against the wind on the Test in Hampshire, lost an eye when his fly made a vicious swing-back into his face. At Testwood, just below the beat where His Excellency lost his eye, I gave a warning to a guest of my own that if a fresh fish took him and ran downstream through a narrow bridge at the tail of the pool, he had no choice but to throw his rod into the water. We could recover it in the shallow below.

In his excitement, when a fish new from the sea struck him like a cannonball, he tried to stop him. Worse, he tried to check the line. As the fish ran downstream, the silk seared through his fingers like a red-hot iron, cutting him to the bone. In his pain, and fortunate it was that he did this, he dropped his double-handed rod. The fish, he was a fifteen-pounder, carried the rod under the bridge into the rough water. We recovered it among the rocks with the fish still on. It was a helluva fight, but we killed the salmon in the end about fifty yards downstream.

In happier circumstances, I remember fighting another fish on a Highland river in water which was so low that most of the time, after I had hooked him, he was slithering about with his hog back out of the water. I knew that I had no chance unless I went in after him. I plunged into a pool which was deeper than I knew. The water filled my waders and anchored me on the bottom. I fought that fish, struggling in a few inches of water in the rocky shallows all about me, myself chest deep as if I were the creaking pivot of a roundabout. I got him in the end but I had to use my gaffe over my shoulder, lifting up to my head to get a hold on him. Then I had to get myself out. Nevertheless, soaked to the bone, I have seldom felt more triumphant.

In my fishing life I have had more than my fair share of luck. Another time, on the middle reaches of the Aberdeenshire Dee, which I understand has the second fastest current of any river in Britain, I hunted into the stream, almost up to my armpits, to reach the fish which I knew were lying under the swirl of water on the opposite bank. To ride the press of water which runs in the Dee, you need literally to sit on it, and to judge every pace you make over the slippery round boulders under your waders. In those days I was fool enough, and young enough, not to bother with a wading staff.

A big fish took me, as they often do, as my line was swinging about 45° downstream of me in the current. He had me off balance on his first run. I was too deep in the water to control my reel properly. I went with him. Stumbling over the cursed boulders on the bottom, I struggled to edge my way into shallower water. At times my boots lost touch with the bottom altogether.

The voice of the ghillie, who I learnt afterwards was howling to me from the banks to cut the line, never reached me. But bit by bit, half swimming, I edged towards my own bank as the fish carried me downstream. My waist-high waders were filled with water. I had swallowed quite a lot. But the weight of the water kept me the right way up.

I had hooked the fish well; otherwise I should never have held him. Most of the time, my rod point was under the surface. But at last I found a slab of rock and got a foot lift which raised me out of the full push of the current. I beat the fish which had so nearly beaten me.

The ghillie, I think, had given me up for lost because he was somewhere upstream and nowhere to be seen. I put the rod over my shoulder and ran the fish ashore up the sloping bank. It's a risky thing to do but it often works. I enjoyed my drachm after that adventure.

I knew a fellow angler who had a long white scar across the palm of his hand caused by a heavy salmon hook cast by another fisherman round a bend in the river. The other angler thought he was into a fish and pulled. And I know another, who in a high wind collected a hook in the lobe of his ear in Galway. The Irish doctor, when my afflicted friend had searched him out, laughed and laughed. 'You all come to me,' he said. 'That'll cost you a pound.'

I once won five pounds by making a bet that I would catch a fish within three casts. I didn't cheat. I revealed that the evening before, about a certain rock, a salmon had plucked me twice. 'I am going to have him now,' I said. I reduced the size of my fly, always a wise thing to do, from a No. 7 to a No. 5. I had him, and my five pounds, on the second cast. James Robertson Justice promised me a bottle of champagne – we would have drunk it anyhow – if I could hook a sick trout, as black as Anthony Eden's hat, out of the millpool beside his house at Whitchurch in Hampshire. It was a big old brownie, not only black but blind. I got him by doing everything you must not do in trout fishing (although it works with grayling). I splashed a fly on the water until the sheer noise of it attracted the attention of the unhappy fish. He rose and grabbed it. I seem to remember that the champagne we ultimately drank was corked. We changed over to malt whisky diluted with Highland burn water, which James used to carry south from his home in

Sutherland in vast jars. A big man, he did everything in a Falstaffian way.

Still, of all the hazards of fishing, I know none to compare with one which befell a shooting pal of mine named Lionel Dunlop, who was concerned with the seed firm of that name in Reading. He, too, was a keen fisherman. He was courting a young woman named Peggy, whose people had some fishing on their place in Scotland. There wasn't much hope of a fish. Lionel took out a light trout rod expecting that his greatest enjoyment would be the company of his girlfriend. But instead he got into the fish of a lifetime. The salmon made a joke of his flimsy split-cane rod. He stuck at it. He stuck at it hour after hour, until the light failed and the fish was only just beginning to tire. At last, in almost total darkness, he got it to the bank. He only had a landing net fit to lift out a three-to-the-pound brownie, but he was determined that he was not going to be beaten.

'Peggy,' he said, 'you will have to take your skirt off to get this fish in.' So she did. Together, in Peggy's skirt, they landed it. When they arrived home, in triumph, the upright-and-downright parents were horrified. The girl had stripped, as they regarded it, in the company of a strange man. They insisted on what was almost a 'shotgun marriage'.

I am glad to tell you that Lionel and Peggy lived together happily ever after.

15

FISHING IN IRELAND

The most amusing place to fish in the world – the people are more
entertaining than their salmon and trout – an expedition remini-
scent of Jerome's *Three Men in a Boat* – the priest who was fishing
for the Reverend Mother at the Convent – pierrot show off Galway Bridge – the Celtic attitude to life – Daddy Longlegs on Lough
Corrib – the 'pocheen'.

As a fisherman I have had little luck in Ireland, except in sea
fishing. There, the massive beasts are huge and hungry.
Fishing from a boat, I have had enormous catches of pollock
and bass taken on a split rubber eel, but I have failed to
master the game fish in the rivers. I have always done well
in Scotland where the fish, so it seems to me, have a stum-
pier neck to their tails. The Irish fish have a finer, more
delicate root, but few of them are tempted by a fly. Such
luck as I have had in Ireland has been with a bait. Yet, no
question, fishing in Ireland is more amusing than anywhere
else in the world.

It is, of course, the people. I arrived in Kilkenny with a
wish to row a boat down one of the slow-running rivers.
The owner of the boat was delighted; but he added that I
would have to wait a while until he painted it. It was only
the day before, when I was staying at the Shelbourne Hotel
in Dublin, that I had asked Paddy the night porter – he is
always Paddy – which floor I was on. He replied, 'Well, you
are not on the first floor, you are not on the second, you are
somewhere between the two.'

A day or two later I had a ghillie in Connemara, improbably named Hastings. Well, not quite improbably. My
family had lived in Fermanagh for about a hundred years. I
asked Hastings what he thought of the weather. He held up
his hand to the sun and remarked, 'It is very hot today. You

had better take your mackintosh with yer.' And, needless to add, he was quite correct.

Immediately after the war, after the discipline of battle-dress, three of us went on a carefree holiday to Galway. It was an expedition as mad as Jerome's *Three Men in a Boat*. At a time when there was still petrol rationing, and food rationing too, we hired a car in Dublin to take us to the West. A delicious colleen stood by as we loaded a battery of rods and tackle aboard. We set out with half a tank of petrol, and, before we had gone half way the needle reported empty. There was no question of filling up again as we cruised over the bogs to our destination. But, accustomed as we then were to battle, we did not care for the morrow. Remarkably the engine kept on turning over.

In the midst of nowhere we were approached by a couple, I suppose that we were drunk, whom we were convinced were leprechauns. In a magical way, they guided us to the fishing lodge we were looking for. The car, apparently with no petrol, actually got us there.

The lodge, as I remember it, belonged to a great land-owner. Although we were supposed to be expected guests, nobody had heard us. There was no food, and no hospitality. The tenant was not alarmed. While we had a dram he disappeared and came back with a basket of sea trout, caught, no doubt, by his own unfailingly successful methods. We had an excellent dinner.

Next day we went fishing on what is theoretically one of the best rivers in West Ireland. One of us – I have written about him earlier – was A. G. Street. He was already a first class fisherman for chalkstream trout. He had never fished salmon. When I saw him on the bank he said, 'Here I am, Mac, £500 of new tackle in my boots. What do I do next?' Unnecessary to add that he ultimately mastered salmon fishing as he mastered farming. But not on our mad holiday in Ireland.

We became alarmed when none of us had caught any fish.

We were all experienced, and we had the benefit of fishing in the best waters in Connemara. I became truly worried, for I had laid fifty pounds to one that between us we would catch a fish before we went home. One of my men said, and indeed wrote in *Country Life* about it, that he would have a better chance of catching a fish with 'Bertie's Bow Tie' than he would with a fly. Bertie was one of us.

The worst came when we were fishing water which I think belonged to one of the Rothschilds, who had invited us as guests. There was a priest sitting with a worm on a home-made rod, over a fall of white water where the sea trout were crowding in. He was whipping them out as easy as knocking off pingpong balls with a rifle in a fairground. We asked him what the hell he was up to on private water. He serenely replied, 'I am catching them for the Reverend Mother at the Convent.'

On that mad holiday in Ireland we did indeed get some fish in the end. In the end, with a fifty to one bet on my hands, I arranged with the lessee who had the netting rights of the fish which run into the pool above Galway Bridge, that one of us should have a go. The man who owned the fishing rights was an Englishman named Cross. He gave permission. It was the easiest fishing in the world because the salmon, which you could see from Galway Bridge, piled up like a queue in a football crowd. Every time you cast a fly you covered fifty of them. I saved my money after a few casts.

The crowd, hanging over the bridge, cheered when the salmon was brought in. My friend who was a surgeon and, like all surgeons, a bit of a show-off, bowed to them. Somebody remarked, 'He thinks that he is a bloody pierrot.'

Years later I went back to Ireland with the intention of filming the remarkable spectacle of the fish crowding to jump the fall, from Galway Bridge. Owing to a trick of light on the water you could see them from the bridge in ranks of dozens, lying there waiting to make the next stage of their breeding run. I was given a hearty welcome by the officials of the Irish Tourist Office, who assured me that the water was still full of fish. By sheer accident, I met an English friend of mine who had just returned from Galway. 'You're wasting your time,' he said. 'There isn't a fish today in the pool.' It turned out that they had been turned away because of a conservation programme by the Water Board to dredge the pool.

Subsequently I believe an enquiry was held in Dublin to discover why I had been told that everything was normal. The officials lied like Irish uncles. I remember a Welshman, another Celt with eyes like a mountain sheep, asking me what I thought of an individual we both knew. 'He's a nice chap,' I said, 'but he's such an appalling liar.' The Welshman looked at me in surprise. 'But he is only lying to please you,' he commented.

Another Welshman, and a famous one, whom I accused of talking nonsense, said to me once, 'How do I know what I think unless I say what I think?' You cannot beat them; but how loveable they are if you take them at their own word valuations.

Lord Killanin who, as I mentioned, is now the maestro of the Olympic Games had all the charm of the Anglo-Irish aristocracy to the free and easy ways of the locals. When he lived in Connemara, he was pals with all the poachers on his excellent stream named the Spiddle. Michael himself joined in by sitting on the top of the falls of his water, which the salmon could not pass, by trailing a worm in the stream below. He passed the time, until a fish took him, reading a good book. He introduced his beautiful Irish wife Sheila to fishing. And he told me that after she had caught her first fish, she woke him in the night, pulling at the hairs on his chest, in a dream that she was having the adventure with the salmon all over again.

I said earlier that I have not had the game fishing success

in Ireland that I have had in Scotland. It is not quite true. On the rivers I have had poor results. But on Lough Corrib, floating the blow line from a boat in the Daddy Longlegs season in the autumn I have brought in good bags of trout, all on the three and a half pound mark. I have had plenty of others on the spoon.

One of the fascinating facts about Corrib, depending where you are in that great lough, is that you can take brown trout in one area whose flesh is pure white and, in another, trout whose flesh is sea trout pink. The shrimp must be locally distributed.

On all my fishing holidays in Ireland, my first memories are of the 'poteen', that formidable and illegal local spirit, always brought out to make up for an empty day. I recollect that, after a dram or two, I went down to fish the river on Lord Killanin's place, where it met the sea. Oh dear, what a bird's nest I had in the dark when I tried to cast three flies. All I remember, as I stood in the water, was that every ten seconds a salmon drove past me in the narrow waters on its way upstream.

But in Ireland it is always the people. It is there, in their company, that you share the charming lunacy of Irish life. In that classic book *Reminiscences of an Irish RM*, the story is told of an Englishman who bought a hunter in the sales. The brute threw him within minutes. The Englishman dragged himself to his feet, and declared it was the best hunter he had ever ridden. An onlooker remarked, 'Faith, he's aisy plaised.'

16

SURPRISES IN ARCTIC NORWAY

How I took the wheel of an Arctic trawler – the Grand Hotel in Hammerfest – where the fish fingers come from – the Lapps and their reindeers – a dreamland for fishermen – the Maelstrom and the Kaiser – the land of sea birds and unexpectedly beautiful girls.

In the land of the Midnight Sun, in the northernmost town of the world, I found myself alone at the wheel of an Arctic trawler. It was all a surprising mistake. I had a notion that I wanted to join in a night's fishing expedition from Hammerfest, the land which, in summer, is in perpetual daylight, in one of the small boats which go out to collect the harvest of cod and coalfish.

Let me say, before I put you to sea, that Hammerfest, with a population of five thousand tough people, only a dozen generations removed from the Vikings, is a place of wonders. On the edge of the polar bear country, they have a stuffed one in the main street which is the mascot of the town. In winter, when there is no daylight, the locals cavort in an indoor swimming pool and an indoor playing ground. The hotel is called The Grand. Nothing remarkable about that. Every other hotel in Norway is called The Grand.

The hotel may not compare with luxury establishments in warmer climates, except in one respect. It is said that but for the beneficent warmth of the Gulf Stream, streaming about the North Cape, no human being could survive in Arctic Norway at all. The locals in that inhospitable climate count breakfast the most important body-warming meal of the day. A breakfast in the Grand at Hammerfest is a feast. The lay-out of the goodies is on a board which stretched from one end of the dining-room to the other.

You can choose eggs, on a serve-yourself basis, cooked half-a-dozen different ways. You can pass on to a choice of a dozen different kinds of bread, a selection of bacon, a vast collection of pickled and fresh fish, conserves and butter, and coffee. One morning I watched two elderly English ladies making a brief sortie from one of the fiord steamships, on what I suppose was the adventure of their lives. They passed from one end to the other of the laden table without putting anything on their plates. At the far end I heard one of them remark to the other, 'No marmalade!'

After that diversion, I still need to explain why I came to be steering a boat in the Arctic Ocean. I was introduced to the skipper, Mr Michaelsen, who spoke, so far as I could tell, only one word of English. It was 'steer'. My interpreter, who himself had only one or two words of English to his credit, somehow got across the message that I was a person who knew about the trawling business. Shortly after we had cast off, Captain Michaelsen grunted 'steer', and retired with his crew to the nauseous comfort of his ship's saloon, where he and his men contemplated sausages in congealed fat in a frying pan, and clearly thanked their lucky stars that they had an expert on board.

Fortunately, at that time of year, there is perpetual daylight. I leaned out of the window of the deckhouse and made a guess at a bearing. The fiord was spattered with ugly-looking rocks and, whatever I did with the wheel, it wasn't long before the bow seemed to swing in line again with the most dangerous looking hazards growling ahead of me.

Life wasn't made easier by the fact that I didn't know what course I was supposed to be setting. When I guessed that we were entering the open sea, I tossed up in my mind whether to steer starboard or port. I fixed my eye on a small island to port. After an interminable hour at the wheel, the skipper climbed lazily on deck. With a glance about him, he got beside me in the deckhouse and disengaged the engine. He grunted something which sounded like 'good'. By some miracle I had brought the boat to the right place and, to this day, the skipper doesn't know that it was by a miracle I did it.

As the little trawler rolled in the swell he switched on his echo-sounder. His men dropped the trawl and we winched in a vast catch of cod and coalfish, plaice and flounders. Ours was only a little trawler, yet we were up to our waists in fish. When the big ones come in to Hammerfest they unload their catch straight into the Findus factory, which provides most of the employment in the little town. The catch goes in as wriggling white fish. It comes out at the end of the assembly line packeted and labelled. It becomes in minutes what we know as 'fish fingers'.

Only the best cuts are taken for human consumption; the waste is processed as animal feed and fish manure. The cod liver oil is rendered down. Although I have a good stomach as a sailor, it made me feel truly sick to watch big Norwegians drink the cod liver oil as enthusiastically as beer. They thrive on the diet like seals. After watching them I felt like a drink; but Finnmark is, alas, a prohibition country.

It was on another visit to Arctic Norway, in the short days of spring in deep snow, that I encountered an encampment of Lapps – those peoples so clearly related to the Eskimos of northern America – when they were driving their reindeer, on which their whole economy is based, to the sea coast.

One of them took me with him when he sallied forth into the mountains adjoining the Great North Highway, to find his own herd. He wanted a beast for meat, its skin for his family's clothes and its bones for various household tools.

The snow was beginning to melt in the breakup, but the sky was a cloudless blue and we sweated as we climbed the steep hillsides. At intervals, we paused for a draught of the snow water pouring in turbulent streams from the mountains. The Lapp had a lassoo across his shoulders, a dirk knife in his loose belt, and he rolled along in his pointed reindeer skin shoes, stuffed with straw for a sole. I put my mouth into the streams and was sure that I had never drunk champagne which compared with that glorious water, bubbling with oxygen, which tumbled out of the mountains.

At last we found the Lapp's herd – they have marks on all their own. Throwing a big loop from his rope, he caught his beast from behind a tree. What followed was a small miracle. After despatching it with a single thrust of his knife, he dismembered it.

Standing there, towering as I did two feet above him, I wondered how he could ever carry it down the hill. The reindeer weighed much more than he did. I watched him skin it, gralloch and leg it. He carefully poured the loose blood from the carcass into the stomach, which he closed with pine needles. He then bound up all the joints, the entrails and the bones into a square parcel inside the skin, which he bound up with his lassoo. He heaved it on to his back like a rucksack. When we started back to his tents he was doubled under the weight. But, even so, he wandered about on the mountainside picking wild berries for himself.

I haven't told you the whole of the story. When he had killed and dismembered the reindeer I looked at the field of snow in which he had done it. I wonder if any Highland keeper could achieve what he did? There wasn't a drop of blood to be seen. Just footmarks.

Arctic Norway, in many ways so like the Highlands of Scotland (which is why the Free Norwegians were based in Scotland in the war), is a dreamland for fishermen. It is so easy to take big fish that casual anglers abandon their catch on the bank. You don't even need sophisticated tackle.

All you need is an old food tin, big enough to get your fist into, and without a rim on the base because that would interfere with the travel of the line when you made a cast. Inside the open end of the tin, nail a strong piece of wood as a handle. Then wind as much line as you want round the outside of the tin. Use nylon because any other sort of line will get twisted. Attach a weight, float and hook if you are bottom fishing, or a spoon or any other sort of bait you fancy if you are spinning. To cast, all you have to do is to spin the tackle in the air and let go, remembering at the same time to point the tin in the other hand (like the guard of a sword) after the bait as it flies through the air.

I fished with one of these home-made gadgets on that terrifying stream which sailors throughout the Seven Seas know as the Maelstrom, which the Norwegians call the Saltstrommen, and which I call the Death Race of the Arctic. It is a narrow channel, one hundred and fifty yards wide, dividing a huge saltwater lake on the land side and the open jaws of a fiord on the seaward side. When the tide is coming in, the broad shoulder of the sea drives the water at tremendous pressure through the channel into the lake. And when the tide goes out, the weight of water in the lake above squeezes the sea back again and it goes through – gurgling, swelling and tumbling exactly as if someone had pulled out the plug of the biggest bath in the world.

Ships of three thousand tons have been smashed into matchwood trying to ride it. Long ago the German Kaiser thought that his new motor torpedo boats were powerful enough to face even the force of the Maelstrom. He stood where I have stood on the banks, watching his navy make the hopeless attempt. The current tossed his ships away like corks. The couldn't pass the current.

The Kaiser, who was an arrogant man if ever there was one, even ordered his Norwegian pilot to sail against the Maelstrom in the German royal yacht. The pilot said that he would obey orders if the Emperor stood beside him on the bridge, and if he, the pilot, were allowed to go ashore first to make his will. After that, even Kaiser 'Bill' had second thoughts.

The absurd thing is that when you see the Maelstrom from the hills on either side of it, you would think that it was quiet enough to swim in. It isn't until you get within a few inches of the platform of rock at the edge, that you feel as if an express train were brushing past your nose. The gullet of water is passing at a rate of 17,500 cubic yards a second.

The depth is a sheer drop of 150 to 180 feet. The pace of the water on the surface is well over thirty miles an hour. Down below it behaves like a charge of maddened horses. But, twice in every twenty-four hours, when it's slack tide, the channel is quiet. Then, provided you take good care to study the tide tables and the balls on the signal mast, you can slip through in a rowing-boat, or even swim in it. Some have.

But what a paradise for fish. There's nothing that a big coalfish or a cod seems to like better than riding the switchback of the wild current. Pulling them out, your only care is to make sure that the nylon line doesn't score your fingers. If they are too hot for you, you only have to walk about a couple of hundred yards to fish sea trout in one of the freshwater streams.

Salmon, especially in the season of the Midnight Sun, are difficult in Norway. You can see every fish in the clear pools in the rivers. The fish can see you. You need to crawl on your navel along river banks to cast a fly, even in twilight, without giving yourself away.

I love Norway. I came home after one visit thinking that we ought to introduce their four-sided open fires into homes in this country. Centred on a chimney in the middle of the room, they throw out heat from a pyramid of logs. An architect pointed out to me, however, that in this country it wouldn't work. The reason simply is that all our own domestic furniture is based on a settling of seats about a fire in one wall.

Of course he was right. Every country has its own idiosyncrasies which would be out of place, however charming, anywhere else. Norway, for instance, still enjoys far more than we do, lonely places.

I remember invading the island of Röst, at the foot of the Lofoten group, where the only inhabitants except a few sheep are puffins, guillemots, gannets and gulls. As I climbed the rocks, searching for a handhold, I had to push the guillemots out of the way. I found heaps of the down of the eider duck in the artificial nests which the Norwegians make for them. I slipped about happily on my bottom on grassy slides which permitted no other way of descent. I seem to remember that on the boat home from the lighthouse I had a memorable dinner of the guillemot's eggs.

But, best of all, I treasure a memory in the Lofotens, that broken-toothed line of islands which adjoins the mainland, when I encountered a lumpy figure in yellow oilskins gutting fish, as they do in Norway, to dry on the line. I explained that I wanted a photograph. The figure, who looked like something out of 'Doctor Who' in that bleak landscape, threw back its hood. There was revealed a tumble of silver blonde curls. Under the oilskins was a white rose of a girl who would have bowled over James Bond. The Norwegians have fish, of course they have. But they also number among their kind some of the most exquisite girls in the world.

17

DOGS IN MY LIFE

My black cocker, Ruins – Tim Sedgwick, the magic dog handler –
the days when Ruins gave me a false point – sex-pot Tessa, my
springer bitch and her pups – the new puppy, Rupert.

A man of the world asserted that in a full life, dismissing
casual encounters, there are six important women. I leave
you to judge the matter. I am bothered, considering all the
dogs which have passed through my hands, that I gave my
full heart to only one dog.

He was a black cocker who was one of the best springers
of game I ever had, though he was a lousy retriever and
hopelessly wild. I named him Ruins not, as it turned out,
altogether without promise of his future character, but
because he was born in the ruins of Cowdray Park, at
Midhurst in West Sussex.

I never had a dog who marked game like him. He had a
style of footwork whether he was pointing a pheasant, a
rabbit, a covey of partridges, or even an adder. We had a lot
of adders on the place I had at that time. I suspect that, at a
period when he was surprisingly ill, he had been bitten by
one. We never proved it but, subsequently, when he
scented an adder he had a technique of advancing and
making a quick wide-eyed retreat. He used to give me the
sort of look over his shoulder to tell me to advance the
safety catch of my gun. On Ruins' instruction I shot many
of them, usually those coiled up at the entrance to a rabbit
bury.

Now that I am reluctant to use a gun, I would never shoot
at anything which deserves a place in the world. But in my
youth the viper seemed an enemy, albeit not an aggressive
one. A naturalist once appeared in our area to offer the local
boys a few pennies for their young. He was overwhelmed

with the collection produced from the local compost heaps, slow worms and grass-snakes' eggs as well.

Ruins was clever enough to catch many a pheasant, usually a hen who stuck too tight in a hedgerow. On one occasion, in deep snow hardened by a heavy morning frost, he got a partridge. When the rest of the covey took off from the place where they had jukked, they left most of their tail feathers behind them. Of course I cursed him. But Ruins was a law unto himself.

And I was not entirely innocent of crime. One twilight night I was waiting for teal. As the last light was going, an arrowhead of birds came in to settle on the pond I was watching. I got a right-and-a-left. Ruins, surprisingly for him, retrieved them both. To my horror I had shot a brace of green plover. I remember that they ate well.

I have known many shooting men whose dogs were always better behaved than mine ever were. One retriever of mine was sent in to pick up a runner, and he came back with an escaped budgerigar in his mouth. But Noel Sedgwick, a former gamekeeper and editor for many years of the *Shooting Times*, all of *his* dogs were wonders.

There was an occasion when we were shooting together on the Berkshire Downs. He looked at his Labrador and remarked, 'Have you come without the beer? Go back and get it.' The dog swung on his rudder and disappeared. I have no doubt that Tim, as we all knew him, had made an arrangement with the publican down below. But in due course the dog came back with a bottle of light ale. Tim scowled at him and said, 'Do you expect me to drink without a glass?' The dog turned, and came back with a glass.

But Tim could work miracles with dogs, all the dogs he ever had. And he could work miracles himself. Although he was no stylist with a gun, I scarcely ever saw him miss. He shot in the way he used a catapult, an art in which his performance was incredible. He normally had a catapult in his pocket. One of his party tricks when he was in a pub, which was often, was to shoot from the hip and shatter a glass on a shelf at the far end of the bar. None of the barmaids could ever discover how it happened.

On another occasion the wife of a guest of mine at a partridge shoot shot a squeaker pheasant. Her husband was very angry with her. But not long after, he himself brought down a carrier pigeon. Tim Sedgwick ran to pick it up. By the time he returned he had plucked the bird and, giving it to my friend, also handed him the aluminium number plate off the bird's leg. 'Here is the wedding ring to go with it,' was his comment.

But I began by telling you about that other personality, my dog Ruins. Impossible though he was in many ways, he never told a lie on a point. Normally when he signalled me, I knew exactly what to expect. I never wasted time putting ferrets into a bury when he did not give me a mark. I think I knew whether he was pointing a cock or a hen pheasant. He was marvellous at showing me the boggy places where a woodcock was at home. But sometimes he failed me.

I could not understand why there were occasions when he gave me a clear signal on the edge of a piece of bramble, or a clump of bog cotton, and nothing showed. At last, I told an old West Sussex countryman about it. He said to me, 'The next time it happens, watch carefully. You will see a jenny wren flit out. Wrens have a game scent.'

Ruins lived for over fourteen years. In human terms that means he lived into his late nineties. I took him out shooting after grey squirrels one February. He kept his head in the air to mark them; he knew the rules of the season. When I brought him home he ate a good dinner, and afterwards the two of us sat in front of the open fire. When I looked at him later that evening he was dead. I was reminded of a formidable uncle of mine who was himself a great hunter during his life. In his mid-eighties, he drove his car on a tour of Spain. On his way home to England, at Angoulême, he dined and lit his pipe. He suddenly said that it had been 'the best holiday I have ever had'. His pipe dropped out of his mouth and, like Ruins, he himself passed on his way.

Sporting friends of mine, like Tim Sedgwick, have attached themselves to black Labradors. Although I have had a few, in particular the close-coupled line with a handsome otter tail, which they fancy in Norfolk, I have never had any luck with them. They were all impressively obedient. I never had one riot like Ruins. But those I have had had no courage in covert. Earlier I had a Clumber, the breed well-loved by King George V, whom I called Jorrocks. He was unexpectedly gun-shy. In latter years I have shared my life with a black and white springer bitch named Tessa. Although I have never shot over her, she is really quite a girl.

Soon after she had achieved puberty, with a family tree of field trial winners as long as anything in *Burke's Landed Gentry*, she was ravished in the woodshed by a yellow dog who passed as a retriever. It was the sort of misalliance which, after all, is not uncommon even in the top company in Burke. But, as usual, it was wretchedly embarrassing to have it happen on home ground.

I found Tessa in her box in the kitchen, trembling with emotion and showing the tell-tale signs that she had lost her virginity. My wife thought that it might have been Skip, a terrier of uncertain origin who belongs to our local doctor. But Skip, I thought, had ambitions above his station. I only had to glance at the yellow dog, lurking outside the barn with his tongue lolling in satisfaction, to be certain that he was the culprit. Something had to be done, and quick; as the limerick goes, 'to save the family's face'.

Within hours, the vet had given Tessa an injection to abort her, promising only that in seventy-five per cent of cases it worked. I told him that we had never been able to work out the rhythm of her heats. No six-months interval for Tessa. She was a sex-pot, who seemed to attract every loose dog in the neighbourhood. 'Next time she comes on,' said the vet, 'you must mate her properly. The bitch needs puppies for her own health.' We didn't have long to wait.

The local dogs were hanging about hardly before we had got over the first emotional crisis. In the local, the wiseacres advised me to count carefully from the beginning of the heat to the twelfth day. I didn't know where to begin counting from. Apart from that, my wife and I have an appointment life of our own. If the twelfth day hit our other engagements, we were in real trouble.

Peter Moxon, of the Beoley Kennels at Redditch, advised me to go to a sire in Berkshire, not far from our own home in Hampshire. But his owner, at the vital time, was taking her dog to Scotland for the shooting. So we had to make the run to Worcestershire – one hundred miles each way – to meet Bekesbourne Peter, a liver and white whom Moxon decided would be an appropriate mate.

As events turned out, the meeting was beautifully timed. Tessa was ready for Peter, and Peter was anxious for her. My wife attended Tessa during that dreary period, in the coitus of dogs, when they are tied together while the semen impregnates the womb. I suppose the animals in their way enjoy it, as I enjoyed a whisky and soda with the breeder.

Moxon said that when she pupped there was nothing to worry about. 'Stay up all night if you want to; but, if you leave her alone, you will probably find that she has got the litter, and cleaned them, before you shave in the morning.'

Oh dear! How I wish these experts were always right. What they don't allow for is a large country family in which there is more excitement about the prospect of a litter of pups than a telephone call from a nursing home about a new baby. Tessa nearly gave us the first shock when, after we had got her home, happy and fulfilled, she somehow sneaked out for a rendezvous with the horrible yellow dog. I drove desperately about the village to find her. I had heard of 'split litters'. I ironed myself, when the time came, to eliminate the bastards. We got her home, the wanton, happy as Reilly with her two lovers that day.

In retrospect, it seems absurd that after adventures like that, after paying the sire's fee, we should have wondered whether she was in pup. Within a few weeks it was evident that she was unusually affectionate; as if in some way she appreciated that we had all shared in achieving what she most wanted. She rolled on her back, the way spaniels do, to invite us to rub her stomach. Her teats began to stick out like spikes on a buckler. She grew huge.

When her time was near, my wife and I had to go away for forty-eight hours, leaving our elderly nannie in charge of the situation. While I was making a speech at a literary lunch in Yorkshire, my wife called home. Nannie reported that Tessa had been crying all the night before, so she had stayed up, as nannies do, cossetting her. Through driving rain from the north we drove back to our farmhouse. When we turned off the engine of the car in the garage, somewhere near midnight, we both heard the whining of a puppy in the stable next door. After a surreptitious peep, we went to bed happy that Tessa would have all her family during the rest of the night.

There had been bets in the house as to where she would choose to have her puppies. Jack, our part-time gardener, was convinced that she would pick the stable. Mrs Seedsman, our housekeeper, thought that she would prefer her favourite retreat behind the boiler. Nannie, hopefully, suggested that it would be under one of the children's beds. They were all wrong. Tessa picked a site beside the deep freeze in the toolshed.

In the morning there were two puppies. As the hours went by, Mrs Seedsman, with maternal authority, told me that in her opinion, there wouldn't be any more. Looking at Tessa, I couldn't believe it. I thought she was distressed. I called the vet again, this time represented by a charming woman practitioner. Tessa seemed to know at once that we were there to help her. I heaved her on to the deep freeze so that the vet could search her inside. Tessa, as I held her, never moved even when she cried with pain.

The vet said, 'There are more, but I think that they are all dead.' We rushed the bitch in for a Caesarean. An hour later I got a call that the puppy, who was the wrong way round inside her, was dead. But there were seven others in the assembly line, all in good nick, and would I collect them because they were making such a noise in the surgery. So I had nine.

It was incredible that when I collected Tessa, just out of an anaesthetic with ten stitches in her stomach, she hopped into the car the way she always does to sniff the additions to her family in a cardboard box beside her. Subsequently, she patiently tolerated all the interference from my own.

With a litter of pups safely, if expensively, delivered, I hoped that was the end of the matter. The vet came to remove two of the remaining nine, reckoning that seven is as much as a bitch with eight teats can do well. Counting her teats – the whole family joined in on that reckoning – she had nine, eight operational. So she ought to do seven splendidly. The tips of the tails of the puppies – just the tips, as field trial spaniels ought to be docked – were done.

The trouble was the jealousies that emerge in a household like ours. Our nannie was determined that nobody, except her, was qualified to handle the new family. She fed Tessa on raw eggs, best steak, milk and cream every few hours. She ticked off her own small charge at any time when she put her nose into the stable. I discovered my seven-year-old daughter in a conspiracy with her friends to remove one pup she called Pluto out of sight of any one who was concerned in making a choice of litter. I had to defeat that. There was competition, Tessa included, to make beds for the newcomers. Even my wife was a little broody.

★　★　★

After attaining the age of twelve, my daughter announced that she wanted a puppy 'of her very own'. I was not surprised. At that age girls want either a pony or a puppy. It is a matter of first love and the budding of maternal instinct. I pointed out that she was just on the brink of going to boarding school. If she had a pup it would be one that, throughout most of the year, Daddy and Mummy would have to look after 'on their very own'.

My wife made a token resistance. But I recognised that look in her eyes which women always have at the prospect of another baby in the house. I knew that I was on to a loser. I argued that we already had Tessa. After her tumultuous maternal career, I had achieved, with the willing aid of our nice local vet, a quieter middle life for her, when all the dogs in the neighbourhood were not crowding about our yard as if it were a brothel in Pompeii. With due solemnity I had fixed the admonitory notice CAVE CANEM on our back door to let it be known that the last days were over. Now the volcano was about to strike again.

With weakening purpose I protested that we already had Matthew, our huge and wicked neutered tabby, who might have been the prototype of Kipling's 'Cat Who Walked by Himself'. I said that if we had a puppy, the young thing would regard it as his responsibility to chase Matthew out of our cave. But my wife, like the first caveman's wife, was wielding the old magic. A puppy, she said, would make Tessa young again. Our Harriet, when she was home, would learn a sense of responsibility looking after it. It would give me personally some much needed exercise. And finally, Harriet had promised to get all the necessary dog leads and insecticides and arrange whatever inoculations the puppy required. It was not, of course, mentioned that the items would all be on my account.

It was clearly foolish of me to bring Tessa into the discussion. She was now just 'a little old lady passing by'. I did not have any strong feelings about Matthew. If the new puppy chased Matthew out of my best armchair when the grimalkin was warming himself sybaritically in front of the fire, I should not be sorry to see him driven into the top branches of the apple trees.

Thus battles are lost. I found myself fearing that Harriet might settle for a bit of pike bait like a Yorkshire terrier, a Pekingese, or one of those temple dogs from Tibet. I was wrong. As soon as I mentioned Tessa, my wife and daughter ganged up on me in the confidence that they had the answer. What they both wanted was a puppy like Tessa. It had to come from the same kennels in Redditch, where all the needles in the world come from too. It had to be black and white. And it had to be one of Peter Moxon's strain.

My wife telephoned. Yes, Mr Moxon had a black and white puppy like Tessa which was ready to go out into the world. All he had against him was that, furniture-wise, he had Queen Anne legs. Naturally, that didn't count with my womenfolk at all. They wanted him. It turned out on the pedigree that Tessa was Rupert's great-aunt. To the delight of my family, they looked like mother and son.

And so, after a trip to the environs of Birmingham, we got them both. We have now discovered that with Rupert's Queen Anne legs, he has a predilection for chewing up the stretchers in Queen Anne chairs. I knew from the start that we could never win. Heaven knows how he came to be called Rupert. Whatever qualities he has, he has nothing in common with the great Cavalier of the Civil Wars. But he wages a war, as pups do, of his own.

The essential difference between one quiet old bitch and one virile dog is the difference between a warm old friend and a pack of hounds. Now I cannot move about the house, even to the lavatory, without dogs nuzzling my calves. They come up to our bedroom in the morning to put their dirty paws on the sheets and their wet noses on my bare legs. They come asking for walks when I am writing things like this. They pay me back, when I am not in the mood for walks, by devastating the house.

My wife is totally forgiving. She seems to regard it as a triumph when the puppy has not done his big business on the kitchen floor at the crack of dawn in the morning. One of us, it is usually she, has to scuttle down in dressing-gown and bedroom slippers to let the puppy out before he hears the call of nature.

We have come to accept – no, my wife accepts – that it is the privilege of puppies to rip the paint off the walls and to tear any fringe off the upholstery of soft furniture. By and large I suppose we are lucky that the little beast has not, as the Americans say, gotten around to shoes. Instead he favours stockings, socks and tights.

He has even done better than that. His particular speciality is eating the post and the newspapers. I can just about do without the newspapers which, expensive as they are these days, are so remarkably gloomy; but the loss of the post can be alarming. Rupert's contribution up to date is to eat a fat cheque from William Hill in payment of a long-priced double, which one of my family won on the flat. He has also stomached another lump of thick paper, covered with stamps, which came to conclude a transaction in shares from the stockbroker. He has eaten several catalogues and circulars which don't matter. But, morning after morning, I and Mrs Smith, the nice woman who does for us, have to sit down to the assembly of a jigsaw of scraps to discover what has been lost that morning.

I have stuck notices on the back door for the attention of the postman and the newspaper boy, with pitiful appeals to them not to throw newspapers and magazines on the floor. 'The puppy eats them'. I have provided a big cardboard box marked LETTERS HERE, in the hope that a cheque to pay off my overdraft will not end up in the puppy's belly. I can record only a half success.

He is now qualified for his first dog licence at the very

reasonable price of seven shillings and old–fashioned sixpence. I hesitate to reckon what he has cost us up till now.
He already needs a bigger collar. My daughter, dedicated to
a puppy 'of her very own', is of course currently busy at
school.

18

ODD BIRDS

Meeting the hoopoe, the 'cock, the quail, the short-eared owl, the stone curlew, and the white blackbirds of Kensington Gardens – a phenomenon in Canada – bats and nightingales – various, including J. Arthur Rank, Captains Knight and Ackland, Henry Williamson, James Robertson Justice.

I am fortunate that I have met a variety of odd birds. Of the avian sort, I have seen that rare visitor to England, the hoopoe, lift his crest to me in the White Water at Odiham in the meadows of Hampshire. I have had the excitement of finding a woodcock's nest in one of the few places in this country where they breed, in Verdley Wood near Fernhurst in West Sussex. I have actually seen a 'cock roding down a ride in twilight carrying one of her chicks between her legs.

I have had the joy of flushing a bevy of quail. On a shooting party at Compton on the Berkshire Downs, we were walking a field of linseed after partridges. The adults got up, with a family as enchanting and just as big as bumble bees following behind them. I stopped the shoot. When we made a circle we had the good luck to see them about three times. It was a year just after Hitler's war, when some of the migratory birds had escaped the Arabs in the Eastern Mediterranean and the Italians on Capri with their beastly nets. I subsequently saw a singleton. But, after that year, never since.

It was on that same shoot, in the plough in winter, that we used to encounter short-eared owls. I never understood what they were doing there, lying flat on their breasts in the cold earth among the hares. I made sure that no gun-happy guest of mine raised his gun to them.

I made sure, too, that nobody lifted a gun to those beautifully coloured birds, the stone curlews. We had a lot of them on the chalk Downs, those same birds which Beach Thomas defined as 'thick-kneed plovers'. W. H. Hudson also studied them over the same land, which ultimately became my sporting domain. Hudson was primarily working out his theory that the rooks and the jackdaws flight along the lines of old forest lands which have long since disappeared. While I was wandering over the Berkshire Downs I never had any cause to disagree with him. The homing rooks, with jackdaws trumpeting them in, sing the song of history.

No doubt that the study of birds is one of the most rewarding of small hobbies. When for a time I was encompassed by London streets, I exercised my dog in Kensington Gardens. I remember that an albino blackbird had been reported there, shortly after the war, in the gardens adjoining the Palace. He must have been a virile cock. Up to ten years ago, almost every blackbird in Kensington Gardens had streaks of white. Maybe they still have. Unlike the white lions recently discovered in Africa, they can clearly hold their own.

I have had strange experiences in less settled parts of the world. One day I was walking with a white hunter hundreds of miles from anywhere in the bush of Kenya. As we approached an isolated tree, it suddenly burst with a cloud of thousands of house martins. The white hunter remarked, 'The migrants are collecting earlier than usual. We can expect the rains a fortnight sooner.' He was right. When I got home I wrote somewhere that I expected the house martins to turn up that year a fortnight earlier than they usually did. I had half-a-dozen letters, from people who keep records of that sort, to show that my prophecy was correct.

Stranger still, I remember flying in a small aircraft from Winnipeg in the prairies to the North-West Territories of Canada. It was the time of year which the Canadians call the break-up, the season in which the ice and the snow melt and give way to a wonderful short season of summer. I was astonished, looking down from the little aircraft, to see combine harvesters grumbling over fields which were still flaked with drifts of snow.

What had happened was extraordinary. The snow had come early with the consequence that the corn harvest had not been gathered in. Farmers went bust. In the spring they were astonished to discover that the corn was still there. They turned out the combines to bring in a fat crop.

That is only a part of the story. When the farmers brought the crop in, they were surprised to find that the fields were infested with harvest mice, which are comparatively rare in Canada. The next phenomenon was that owls, from all over the Americas, got the message. They crowded in to eat the harvest mice. Such are the wonders of ecology.

After experiences like that I can believe anything. I was led to believe, for example, that nightingales sing only at night. They don't. In the ardour of my youth I remember making love at noonday, with a nightingale singing sweetly on a branch six feet away.

I have happy memories of a day spent with two enthusiastic batmen in a cave in Dorset, which was full of bats. We found a company of horseshoe bats. Upside down, asleep in the rocky crevices, they looked as beautiful as tulips before they blow. My batmen friends engaged to handle them. They did not manage it as well as I did. One of them got bitten. Horseshoes have a strong bite which, unlike the harmless pipistrelles, can draw blood out of you like Dracula.

I was luckier; or perhaps more careful. I had the television people there. When I brought a horseshoe bat out into the daylight, I was able to tell the camera crew which way he would fly. Of course he curved back into the cave. They got a splendid film shot.

One of the batmen, a civil servant, kept vampires in his terraced house in Basingstoke. He used to come to my farmhouse with a radio device, which he had borrowed from the Ministry of Defence, to check whether I myself had any about the place. I told him I hadn't. He proved me wrong with his machine by picking up the squeaks of pipistrelles, which you are not supposed to hear after your twenties, all about the house. It appeared that I had a colony of the creatures in my loft.

Yet, all said and done, the oddest birds I have met in my life have been human ones. I have fond memories of so many of them.

I think of J. Arthur Rank (late Lord Rank), whom I never knew as a millionaire and tycoon but whom I got to know quite well as a countryman. He had a theory that pheasants were not worth shooting, insisting that they were too easy. So on his estate at Sutton Scotney in Hampshire he cultivated partridges, so much so that he ruthlessly killed pheasants in September. He had little huts all over his fields to feed and water the partridges, and he took me on a tour in a Land Rover to show me what he had done. Having got into one field, he could not find the way out. In exasperation he finally drove the waggon through one of his wire fences. 'Never mind,' he said, 'I pay for them.'

Impoverished person that I am, it is funny that I have had so many contacts with millionaires. Maybe they draw to me, or me to them. Perhaps they recognise that I do not want their money. Another tycoon I knew was Tony Vanderfeld, a big man in motor cars. One day he turned up for an evening's mayfly fishing on the Kennet, with a car the like of which I have never seen before. It was as beautiful as a ladybird and, remarkably, it opened like a ladybird. There were no conventional doors; at the touch of a button it raised its wings. I was most impressed by it – and so were the cows in the field.

When Tony and I had set off to fish the mayfly hatch, the cows crowded round and successfully licked six layers of paint off the wonder motor car. The reduced a half of it to bare metal. I laughed, but Tony the millionaire did not think it very funny. You have to be poor to enjoy the embarrassment of the very rich.

The odd birds in my life have been precious. Captain Knight used to lunch with me with a hawk on his fist in, of all places, Fleet Street. He reminded me of a falconer in a cartoon in *Private Eye* who, unloosing his fly buttons with an evil-looking hawk on his wrist, evoked the caption: 'Aren't you taking a bit of a chance?'

I used to know Captain Ackland, who nursed a strange notion that cuckoos are all males who cuckold the pipits and the other song birds into mothering their eggs. He believed that there were no female cuckoos. Apart from this strange notion, he was not a bad naturalist.

One of the keenest shots I ever encountered was a man who, by common consent, had never killed a bird. He let off his gun with gay abandon at everything that passed over him. I fancy that all the pheasants and partridges knew, when they saw his number on the card, that they were safe as houses. It was obvious, to nobody's disadvantage, that he enjoyed his sport. He blinded off to no effect into the air. Not for him to calculate the waste of cartridges.

Another amiable eccentric I knew could successfully upset any drive. As soon as the birds were whistled over, he shouted down the line, 'They're on your left. They're on your right. Look at that old cock behind you. Mark it, it's a woodcock.' He confused so many guns that they shot wildly. His boast over luncheon was to invite anybody who bothered to listen again to look at his eyelids. He had two pellets, collected on two separate occasions, lodged in one of them, and he was too proud to have them removed.

There was another character who blew off his toes with his first barrel and shot a partridge with his second. Subsequently he had to be removed on a stretcher.

All right, I myself have pricked, and *been* pricked once or twice in my life. I have even pricked a beater. On one occasion I inexcusably shot a rabbit in front. A ricochet went through a beater's gumboot. In crawling apology I gave him a pound, which in the days it happened was quite a lot of money. He grinned at me and said, 'Do it again!'

But of all the rare birds, I count Henry Williamson the author, and James Robertson Justice the actor, as two of the most remarkable people I have shared the field with. Alas, they have both died quite recently; and both celebrated in memorable memorial services; one at St Martin in the Fields in Trafalgar Square, the other at the mediaeval chapel of St Cross in Winchester.

Henry was a friend of nearly forty years' standing. It is useless to pretend that he was an easy man to get on with for he was completely lacking in any sense of humour. He drove through life with an intensity of purpose which was quite alarming. By way of example, I remember a time when he asked me up to North Norfolk, where he then had a farm, to shoot wildfowl on the saltings.

At the crack of dawn we set out together for the tideline. Half way there, over the mud and the coarse grass, he sat down on a tussock. 'I can't go any further,' he said dismally. 'It reminds me of Flanders Field.' I went on without him; and, incidentally, when the tide came in, like running horses, I was jolly lucky to get back with my birds and my gun without calamity.

Henry was obsessed with his experiences as a young man in the misery of the trenches in the First World War. He wrote a dozen books about the time. Under my breath, I doubt whether he was a good naturalist, but what he had was a wonderful imagination.

He was a puzzling man. Women loved the blue-eyed dreams he brought to life for them. My own humanity was shocked when he nailed a heron's beak to one of the beams of his farmhouse. His moods were unpredictable. I wish that I had got on better with him: so did most of his contemporaries. In his more exasperating moments he had a taste for schoolboy mischief, in which he behaved like *Just William*. At other times he could string himself up emotionally to the point of tears. He was a genius who was best known, at a distance, in his books. In his memory, I treasure a walnut tree he grew from a nut and which he gave me in a little pot. I planted it in my own cottage garden. It is now a splendid specimen, big enough for Henry himself in one of his giant-killing moods, to climb.

By contrast, I think of James Robertson Justice, another romantic, as one of the joyous people I have known in my life. He was never far removed from Falstaffian laughter. In later life he achieved fame as a film star, but he would have preferred to be remembered as the superb practical naturalist which Henry Williamson was not. Henry was ruled by what his mind wanted to see. James saw with eyes so sharp that even a little pipit couldn't conceal her nest from them.

If James had ever met Henry they would undoubtedly have hated each other's guts. Without entering into detail, I have a shrewd notion as to the sort of political explosion that would have occurred. For my part, I took care that I never brought my two friends together.

Henry, with his conspiratorial voice, and James with his bellowing one would have been oil and water. Remembering James, I recall the verse that the Victorian poet, Austin Dobson, wrote on visiting the tomb of Samuel Johnson:

> Ye Gods, how he talked
> What a torrent of sound
> His hearers invaded, encompass'd, and drowned

Thus it was with James. In his public image, from the great drum of his chest, he invaded conversation. In his private one, in the quiet of his lovely home overlooking the Dornoch Firth in Sutherland, he was a different person. Indeed, he was a very modest one.

He had a great reputation, outside his films, as a falconer. He loved falcons, he cossetted them all his life, and intellectually he knew everything about manning them. But he was not clever with his handling. The hawks wouldn't settle with him. He only had to take a peregrine on his fist to have the bird baiting. In his successful days in films, he hired Philip Glasier, a man with yellow eyes like a hawk himself, to manage his birds for him. It worked better that way.

It was odd that temperamentally, James and his beloved birds never seemed to suit each other. He had them line up on their blocks outside his house. He carried them in his Land Rover through the Highlands where he wore his Robertson kilt, the kilt which he insisted should never be donned south of the Highland Line except on one day a year. What the day was I never discovered. All I remember is that one evening in Hampshire I met a spruce little man whom James, from his own great size, flamboyantly introduced me to as his father. By way of making conversation, I asked Mr Justice whether he had been to Scotland lately. 'Scotland?' he enquired indignantly. 'Never been to the place in my life.'

James was a Scot by adoption, there are surprisingly many of them, who was a Highlander in spirit rather than origin. He married himself to the hills and exuberantly made them his own. The Scottishness in him, the Robertson in him, was inherited from his splendid mother.

If ever there was a man who filled Kipling's 'unforgiving minute with sixty seconds worth of distance run', it was James. He was quite inconsistent in his enthusiasms. One day it was fishing and shooting. Next he declared that he was tired of all the field sports. A good writer, he began many books and never finished one of them. In the various turns of his life he was racing driver, failed Parliamentary candidate, formidable punt-gunner, and, at last, a film star extraordinary. He was an exquisite linguist in at least three languages, and a good musician. Of course he wailed the bagpipes. But he never wavered, as he did in so many of his human affairs, in his lifelong love affair with his hawks.

When he achieved fame on the screen there inevitably came a time when he accepted a contract for a film in Hollywood. He hated the place. When he was not wanted on the set, he escaped into the Arizona Desert where he passed his time snaring passage hawks with a clap net.

On his return to England, passing through Customs at Heathrow, the officer asked him what he had in a Gladstone bag he had brought with him.

'Hawks,' said James, flinging open the bag and revealing a row of them, duly hooded, on an improvised perch he had fixed into the sides.

'The regulations,' said the Customs officer, 'are pretty strict about bringing in tame birds.'

'They are not tame. They are passage hawks.'

'What did you pay for them?'

'I didn't pay anything. I caught them in the desert.'

'I'm sure you're not allowed to bring them things into this country.'

A senior officer was summoned. Books of regulations were closely examined. There was nothing relevant to wild hawks, unpaid for.

'I'm afraid that we shall have to hold these birds pending further enquiries,' said the bewildered senior of the service.

'What do we feed them on?' enquired his anxious junior.

'Well,' said James, 'I've got some frozen rat meat in my pocket. That ought to keep them going until you sort the matter out.'

'Look here, Mr Justice — we know you, of course — take these bloody birds out of Customs and don't do it again.'

If James reads this in his Valhalla, there's nothing here which we didn't share in laughter in his lifetime. I even used to tell him that his beard, which he tossed so aggressively and to such commercial advantage, concealed the real, deeper man beneath it.

Gosh, I miss him; and Henry, too. Don't believe the nonsense that 'we shall never see their like again'. People like them are as endemic to the country scene as the green grass and the wind in the willows. The next generation will certainly see the likes of those men again.

19

BELIEVE IT OR NOT

The regional hazards of crocodiles and poisonous snakes – a crocodile which bit me – the cobra which bit me – 'The Seven Sisters' – fishing rainbows in the Arctic snows.

The most formidable animal in Africa – you may excuse the elephant, the buffalo, the leopard and the hyena – is the crocodile. If you put your hand in a river in that torrid continent, you do it at your peril. A crocodile has a speed of about forty miles an hour in water and, unbelievably, about twenty miles an hour from a start on land. Native women doing their washing are regularly dragged into the crocodile's lair. Antelopes nosing into the water for a drink are snatched down by the apparently lazy beasts, who strike with terrible speed.

I remember a couple of foolish young men who swam every day in the Zambesi River just above Victoria Falls. They believed that the current was too strong for the comfort of the 'crocs'. At the end of a fortnight, during which they played with the crocodiles' jaws, neither came back. You cannot amuse yourself in that company.

It is said that if you splash about in an African river they will leave you alone. When I have been unbearably hot I have, admittedly, taken a chance, but only in the desperation of cooling myself down.

In my time I have tried to shoot them. Finding them lying like great logs on the bank, I have aimed to hit them with a heavy rifle in their red eyes. I have never recovered a beast that I've shot. With a great kick of their scaly tails, they have always launched themselves into the water to be eaten, no doubt by their own kind.

Only once did I see one pulled back out of the river. It was a relatively small croc, say six feet long, which the hunters got ashore by throwing a noose over its head in thin clear water. In the commercial market, where crocs are harvested for their leather for wallets, handbags and luggage, in places like Lake Victoria, I have been told that they use lamps to draw the reptiles to their doom. I have never seen the operation.

Even if I had the opportunity, I would not shoot a crocodile now. Cruel things that they are, they are the dustmen of Africa's rivers. It is unquestionable that if they were exterminated, and men have tried, the ecology of Africa, the essential balance of nature would be destroyed. In their own horrible way they keep the warm waters clean.

Latterly I caught a baby crocodile in the Chobe, which is a tributary of the Zambesi. He was only about ten inches long, but he locked his jaws across my fingers. It was weeks before I healed. I brought him home in a tin to the London Zoo, where he flourished until he was about five feet long. Looking back, I suppose I ought to have left him where he was.

I was told years ago that of all the hazards to human life in Africa, crocodiles were the most dangerous. I was shown records putting them at the top of the killer list. This may seem surprising, because Africa has more than its share of venomous snakes. But the records I saw made it clear that in Africa, the snakes come among the 'various' in the casualty list.

Years ago, when I traversed the arid country of the Kalahari, I was warned again and again to look out for poisonous snakes: the mamba, the whip of Africa, which is said to have a speed which can outstrip a truck; the puff adder, rather a slow-coach unless you get between him and his hole; and, of course, that very handsome fellow, the king cobra. I was instructed never to put my head down in camp for the night without making sure that there were not a couple of honeymooning cobras under my pillow.

POOR FELLOW: The shikar was delighted when I felled this Indian bison, a rogue from the herd. Weighing about three tons he is the biggest cloven-footed animal in the world. As soon as I had done it I regretted it. But, within the hour, peasant from miles around gathered to collect their morsel of the meat of the great beast. It comforted me that my kill provided food for about three villages.

In national costume on this beautiful Arab in the Jordanian Desert, I went hunting with the Bedouin.

With a cobra for company I became a snake charmer in the market places of Bangalore in Southern India. I was a cheat because the cobra's poison fangs had been drawn.

Neither this camel nor I got on very well with each other. The trick of controlling camels on a sort of side-saddle with the aid of a rein between your toes needs learning.

Elephant are altogether more friendly creatures. But their skeletons are so huge that they move like drunken trams. I was lucky to stay aboard one as he rolled along the jungle tracks.

One of my deviations from powder and shot was to take lessons in the ancient art of archery from Frank Bilson, a former English champion on the lawns of the Royal Toxophilite Society in London.   (see *Bows and Arrows*)

Sharing a coconut with my dog Friday at the end of the adventure when I cast myself away on a desert island in the Indian Ocean a thousand miles from anywhere. It's the nearest I have been to reaching the end of my tether.
(see *The Countryside on Television*)

When I got to the end of my journey one of our District Commissioners asked me how the safari had worked out. 'At any rate,' I said, 'I never saw any snakes.' The Commissioner slapped me on the shoulder. 'You may depend upon it,' he said, 'that the snakes have seen you, my boy.' They obviously tolerated me.

Subsequently in India, I asked for comparative figures with the African rate. In India, deaths from snakebite, cobras especially, were at the top of the list. Deaths from crocodiles were nowhere. I still wonder why.

The Indians themselves are terrified of snakes. It happened that one of my more exotic adventures was to pose as a snake-charmer in native clothes in the market place of Bangalore, in Southern India. I had a basketful of cobras. The snake-charmers' secret is to remove the poisonous fangs (which, incidentally, do grow again). But, handling the snakes, you still need to be careful. I picked up one of mine too roughly and it bit me in the shoulder. It was comparable with a rat bite. But the remarkable thing was that even though there were hundreds of people, with nothing else to do but look at me, I could still keep them all at a distance simply by using my mutilated cobra as a sort of firehose.

I have fished for mahseer in India with a row of crocodiles lazing on the opposite bank, and women beside me in the water up to their thighs, doing their dhobi. They all feared the snakes. Why snakes in Africa seem to be kind in the country where crocodiles kill, and crocodiles in India are kind where snakes kill, is beyond my understanding.

There is so much in my travels about the world which has bewildered me. I wonder what the species of bird is that the Indians call 'The Seven Sisters'. They turn up again and again in the jungle; always seven anonymous looking brown birds. Why seven? There are so many good reasons why a flock should be smaller, or larger. But I promise you that in my experience it has always been seven.

In climactic contrast, I recall the most extraordinary angling expedition I have had in my years was in Yellow-knife, in the Great Slave Lake in the North-West Territories of Canada. I was invited to fish for trout. The snow was still deep on the ground and we set out behind a team of huskies pulling a sledge. We were dressed like Eskimos, furred up to our ears, leathered from top to toe.

We arrived beside the half-frozen river, and the rods burnt our hands in the cold. The half-melted ice in the spring break-up was starting to burst into wild snow water. Great lumps of ice tumbled down the river. Truthfully, I thought that we were wasting our time. We fished, our fingers stiff with cold, with large lake flies; and I have never known trout take like it. There was no art in it. If you could throw a fly into the troubled waters, the rainbows, starved for months under the ice, took like tigers. The problem was bringing them to the bank through the turbulent waters; and I know that I lost many more than I landed. The average weight was two to three pounds.

It was in no sense fine fishing. But it was one of those memorable experiences, denied to men who angle only for the fastidious, educated and selective creatures of our chalk streams. Of course, our own dry fly purists are right to choose the difficult way. The fly fisherman I admire the most is a friend who insists that one big trout in a day is quite enough. But it is still an adventure to fish when they go mad.

20

HUNTING ALONE

Inventing a private field sport – a bit of rabbiting – the only justification for big game hunting – how I did not shoot a lion – 'we always shoot Pierre'.

Much as I have enjoyed shooting in company, I have most relished hunting alone. I fancy that gamekeepers share my own sentiments. The social side of shooting has its charm, but the solitary man discovers a quiet communion with nature which cannot be shared with anyone else.

Perhaps that is the reason why so many gamekeepers I have known have been would-be poets. It has been embarrassing how often Moleskins have pushed bits of crumpled paper into my hand, knowing me to be a professional writer, in which they have expressed their secret thoughts. I have shared them more than they knew.

Deep down inside I, too, am a loner. When all's said and done, my most joyous hours have been those when I have had no more than a couple of brace of cartridges in my pocket, perhaps a few snares, and a good dog at my feet.

I may claim to have invented a private field sport. You cannot play it in heavily wooded, or heavily stocked pheasant country. It is ideally suited to the chalk downs where, in open country, the spinneys are sparse and the game is relatively scarce. The object of the exercise is to spring a cock pheasant. My dogs, who are always wild but reliable finders, never give me a chance when they first put a cock up.

The game is to watch him go over the Downs – my rule is that hens don't count – and make a guess where the old cock has landed in the brook, the brambles, the spindle, or the thin clumps of woods. I play the course like golf. Par for the hole is usually about three. I have known clever old birds who have defeated me six times after a march of maybe six miles. My pride is to mark the plumage of the bird I first sighted, and to make sure that I never let my eye leave the ball. It is a most satisfactory exercise if you have the good luck to be on the sort of course where the game is possible. It is also most economical in the conservation of game.

A lesser sport, which is beginning to revive now that the rabbits are beating myxomatosis, is surely all the variations of hunting the irrepressible coney. There is a story in *Watership Down* by Richard Adams, in which two rabbits say to each other, 'Shall we hold our ground and outnumber them?' It is happening again, although my impression is that the new generation of rabbits are much more cunning than their pre-myxomatosis forebears. They take care not to show themselves on the verges of the fields. They don't use the burrows where the killing fleas wait. They are mostly what we used to call 'bush rabbits'.

But, what sport countrymen have always had from them, and are just beginning to have again. I was always a loner when I went after them, when they infested every field; and A. G. Street made the prophecy that if rabbits could be eliminated, it would be worth two counties to the agricultural produce of Britain. In the event, myxomatosis proved him dead right.

I hunted them with brass snares in Berkshire. I got quite good at setting the snares, arranging them in a tennis-racket shape at the right height at the right place where I marked their jumps. The trouble was that I could never bring myself to get up early enough in the morning to anticipate the fox. He nearly always got there before me.

So I swapped to purse nets. There is no sport which is better practised alone; it is fatal to have others stamping about over the buries. The cocker I had then would creep lightly over them, simply giving me a signal with his boot-button eyes when the rabbit was home. I had two beautiful jill ferrets, little ones, who knew how to bolt without looking for trouble; and it was seldom that I had to call in the old liner to help. I rarely had to dig out. I'd come home with a line of legged rabbits hanging on my graft.

In time, because we were infested with rabbits, I tried long-netting. But I and my friends never had any skill in it. Perhaps our dogs weren't up to the job. Perhaps we had drunk too much when we went out at midnight to make a good catch. In the event, I cannot recollect that we ever caught more than half-a-dozen.

In big game country in Africa I always insisted on going after the quarry alone. There seemed no point in it if the hunter, with all the odds on his side, was insured by half-a-dozen guns behind him. The risk, such as it was, was the primeval charm of the hunt. There isn't even much skill required in killing big game. What you need is nerve. On the occasions when all they have found of the hunter after an encounter with dangerous game is bits and pieces, you may depend upon it that the hunter hadn't drawn his rifle bolt and put it back clean. In fact, he'd panicked. It was said of the best big game shot I ever knew that had he been charged by a wounded beast, he would have had the calm to drop on his hunkers and stop it off the end of his nose.

It is important to add that the man who hunts alone, especially in the whirling sands of Africa, is best equipped with a loose-fitting Mauser-action rifle. It is less likely to jam. The beautifully engineered weapons beloved of Highland stalkers, your Purdeys and the rest, are unreliable in the unforgiving moment when you need to test yourself against a charging buffalo.

In the African bush, that savage country where nature has never yet made up its mind, where trees drop their leaves in different seasons, where rivers flow in different directions from year to year, and where whirlwinds sweep away lumps of landscape, you are in bare fact very much alone.

In my youth I was an eager hunter. On a dawn in the arid wastes of the Kalahari I saw a lion. In that land, lions are reckoned with good reason as vermin. I followed him into the mopani bush which, at that time of year, is bare of leaves. But, as I went on, my gunbearer touched me on the shoulder. The lioness, said the big Zulu, is just behind you. I turned and shot her dead. The trouble was that the lioness was a hyena, as big as a lioness and, by comparison, very ugly.

I was shocked that I had shot the animal, undecorative though he was. I was told afterwards that if I had hung about, the lion would have returned. The hyenas always attend a lion's kill. But my heart had gone out of the sport. I have not shot big game since. Nor will I ever again.

In fact, I belong now to the club of the French sportsman, of whom the story is told that during a barren day, when a hare got up from her form, the host shouted to his English guest, 'Don't shoot. We never shoot Alphonse.' That evening, a hare started up again in the same place. The Englishman held up his gun. 'Shoot, shoot,' yelled his host, 'we always shoot Pierre.'

Nowadays, I think I prefer it that way.

21

SHOOTING WITH A MUZZLELOADER

Looking back on the past – the hazards of shooting in the early
nineteenth century – the dangers of black powder – the care you
must take in firing vintage guns – the greater care you must take in
loading them – looking after them is a messy business.

I have a theory, shoot me down if you like, that the hunting
instinct is closely allied to the sexual one. In the virility of
my youth I was an ardent hunter. In middle age I caught
myself holding back my gun when I thought that the quarry
was too easy. Richard Jefferies, that great country writer,
told how he grew into a mood when he wanted to make
it more difficult for himself as a shot. He went back to the
muzzleloader of our forefathers in the nineteenth century.
So did I.

It was Jack Hargreaves, now the bearded sage of Southern Television, who introduced me to the old guns. Jack has
a more cultivated knowledge of rural life in the past than
anybody I have ever known. I owe it to him, and latterly to
Major Hugh B. C. Pollard that I learnt the dangerous fun of
burning black powder.

It was just what I wanted. I had achieved a certain facility
with a modern 12-bore double-barrelled ejector. I had also
grown into a mood when I preferred to watch the birds fly
over rather than knock them down. With a muzzleloader,
the whole game was far more interesting.

I can write now with the authority of one who has blasted
off his own eyebrows and stripped the skin off his trigger
finger. Anybody who sports with the old muzzleloaders
does so, as the hotel notices have it, 'at owner's risk'. I fancy
that it was always that way. Our forefathers in the sporting
prints in chimney-pot hats – lacking only weepers to mourn
the casualties – accepted the hazards as part of the game.

Today, with every year, the odds on guns blowing up through tired metal and bad expertise shorten. I once had the temerity to fire a flint gun, made by the great English gunmaker Nock in the last years of the eighteenth century. When I fired it, after at least one hundred and fifty years of silence, the gold enclosure of the touchhole blew away and the bead on the foresight dropped off. I would not be writing this if the barrel had burst as well. Richard Jefferies claimed that he used a matchlock. I doubt it. He must have meant a flintlock.

The wiser course is to shoot modern replicas, which are increasingly being made now. It is not to my own taste, in which the fun of the game is to lengthen my own life into the past with the touch of old walnut, Damascus barrels and actions which sing after lying silent for a century.

It is, of course, a risky game. Some of the percussion guns – as members of the Muzzleloaders' Association demonstrate every year at the Game Fair – are in good trim. The flintguns, for obvious reasons, are fewer. But both shoot as far as modern breachloaders, although they take longer to load. If loaded right, every muzzleloader is an individual; they pattern well too.

You can shoot black powder out of aged barrels within the same reasonable margins of safety as you can explode it out of the cardboard case of the firework known as a Roman Candle. Terribly dangerous stuff outside a gun barrel, black powder is relatively innocent within. What you must watch, for the same reason that a squib is twice as lively if you stamp on it, is the weight of the shot put on top.

Nowadays, only an exceptionally preserved muzzleloader could stand a proof charge. I had one once, a double-barrelled flintgun made in Ireland, which actually survived a proof charge of black powder. But such guns are rare. With values rising in the collectors' market, it would be folly to risk a burst in a vintage gun. You must feel your way. If the gun seems in reasonable condition, you can extend the elasticity of the metal by exploding a nominal charge.

The trick is to try an old gun, flint or percussion, by lashing it to the sort of wooden horse which is used for sawing logs. At the end of a sensibly long string, tied to the trigger, it is woken up with a minimal charge. If it survives, the load is increased; but not to the charges recommended by our forefathers in the nineteenth century. In the field you will not do too badly with a 14-bore, now rated as a 12-bore, with a load of a drachm and a half of powder and three quarters of an ounce of shot.

If it is felt that the gun has been exercised enough to chance it on the shoulder, you should load with square-bashing discipline. The heel of the butt should be settled against the boot, the right arm pushed away in the stand at ease position. If it is a double-barrelled weapon, the ramrod is dropped into one barrel, while powder from the flask is poured into the other. This is to obviate the common, sometimes fatal error of double charging. The shooter can test whether the load is well seated by tapping the barrels with the rod.

For regular shooting, always remembering to keep the head clear of the mouth of the gun, the powder should be rammed down hard with an oiled wad, tamping home the charge of shot just enough to hold it in position. A knob of newspaper is admirable for the purpose of holding down the shot charge, just sufficiently to prevent it leaking out of the gun barrel. It provides a satisfying pyrotechnic effect when the gun is fired.

Percussion guns, with modern copper caps on the nipples which will not fly to pieces as they used to in the past, are easily primed. Flint guns call for more care. The seating of the flint, in a wrapping of soft leather, is an art, fixing it so that it strikes the frizzen pan with a fat spark. Getting good flints today is difficult; the sort of flints with which it is said that both sides fought the Battle of Waterloo. The best you can buy are not worth much more than seven shots. But I have had the good fortune at Brandon on the Norfolk/ Suffolk border to meet the knappers who chipped hard black flints to match one of my own guns. The best of them were worth twenty-five shots, and more.

With a muzzleloader it was common, in the excitement of the chase, for men to forget to remove the ramrod out of the barrel. It was a familiar accident, after a hangfire, for a man to blow his head off looking down the barrels to find out what had happened. People who loaded from their powder flasks in too much of a hurry, when there was a spark still winking from the last shot, blew their hands off. But they were a game lot.

Those who indulge today in the eclectic sport should remember that there is a tenth of a second time lag between pulling the trigger of a flintgun and fire. That is why the old prints and woodcuts never show a shooter taking an oncoming bird. They went for going-away flat shots. They also kept their hands uncomfortably back into the fore-hands of their guns because they could not be sure that the barrels would not burst on charge. Shooting was a hazard-ous sport for the shooter until the second half of the nineteenth century.

The old authorities commended all sizes of shot before shot was standardised. Nowadays you should stick with a muzzleloader to Nos. 5 and 6. A woman's hairpin is invaluable for picking out the touchholes after a misfire, and a turnscrew equally so for changing flints. And when you come home, smelling as you will like a dead firework, the gun should be cleaned in a pail outside the house.

The muzzleloaders coke up like old tobacco pipes. You need to pump out the black water in the barrels and blow through the touchholes with cold water, finishing with a kettle of hot water to dry them out. After a libation of oil, they ought to be fit for the next shooting day. The shooter, though, will not be so until he has had a bath.

I confess that I have now parted with most of my antique guns. When I was first interested, gunmakers were delighted to make a present to me of their obsolete stock. I bought powder flasks and shot bags for old-fashioned shillings. I remember buying one old gun for a couple of pounds in which I discovered that nobody had ever drawn the charge. It is all different now. People who are not at all interested in shooting are paying the earth for the remnants of the past. I admit that I have profited from the new collectors' age. But they will never have the fun out of it that I have had.

I still keep a few sporting guns hanging in my hall, made by masters like Nock and the two Mantons. I still treasure a few powder flasks and shot pouches handled by English sportsmen in the past. As Hilaire Belloc wrote, a knowledge of the past may not make a man wise and great, but it brings him into communion with wisdom and greatness, and extends his life far longer than his own.

I have arrived at the cycle in my life when I do not much want to shoot a muzzleloader any more. I even give the fox a fair run when he steals my chickens. When I fish, I put what I have caught back into the water – with the exception of a fresh salmon. Perhaps I will eventually get round to that.

22

BOWS AND ARROWS

The weapon which dominated the battlefields of the mediaeval wars – English yew was an inferior wood for bows – an arrow still has an edge on a bullet out of an Express rifle – learning archery from a modern exponent – the healthiest sport a man or woman can enjoy.

One of my deviations from powder and shot was when I reminded myself that an arrow, silent and true, is still one of the most effective weapons a man can employ. I forget whether it was the wise old Duke of Wellington, or Winston Churchill who asserted that with a company of Welsh bowmen, the Battle of Waterloo would have been won twice as quickly.

Certainly the muzzleloading Brown Bess, which the infantry used at Waterloo, was a wildly clumsy and inaccurate weapon. It took a precious minute to reload. And there was always the unhappy chance that the flint would fail, that the powder was damp and that the gun would misfire.

In the fourteenth century, at the historic battles of Crecy and Poitiers, the Welsh bowmen had it all buttoned up. They were dripping blood with dysentery as they went into battle. At Agincourt it is said that they dispensed with their breeches. They were half starved. But faced with the formidable might of the armoured chivalry of France, they had their yew bows which they could use more effectively than the Old Contemptibles could use their short Lee Enfields in 1914.

It is said that an archer could release ten arrows, perhaps more, in a minute. Their battle orders survived to the First World War, and even into the Second. Their captains gave the order, as the enemy approached, 'Rapid fire'. It is believed, and it is not unlikely, that the first salvo was made with arrows deliberately reduced in length to fall short. It encouraged the opposition to come closer. But when they were in killing range the archers swung their bows high into the air. They rained a whispering murderous shower out of the sky.

At first they let go, their tight bowstrings drawn to their ears, with the inferior feathered arrows supplied by the commissariat. In rapid fire it gave the enemy a taste of what was coming. At close range, one say of fifty to one hundred yards, the order, as it remained up to 1914, was 'deliberate fire'.

The archers picked out of the ground their own personal, carefully feathered and straight arrows, each one marked on the shaft with the bowman's individual colours. The heads of the long arrows, with their killing bodkin-headed shafts, had such penetration that they went through a knight's armour and pinned him to his horse. One arrow could lock two men together. After the battle the bowmen ran forward to claim their quarries. They all knew their own arrows. Just imagine Dai this and Dai that telling his neighbour, 'This is yours.' They shared the plunder.

It is popularly supposed that the yews for the bows were grown in churchyards in England. It is not true. The yews in England were grown because they are poisonous to cattle, to force the farmers to keep their animals out of sacred ground. Our own yew provides at best an inferior bow. The wood for the long bows of England was imported. The best bow wood, the true straight-grained wood, came from the mountains of Europe, especially Spain. The first example of a tariff in England was introduced at the time of Edward III, the father of the Black Prince, who required that for every butt of wine imported, ten bow staves should be paid in duty. It was a wise enactment.

In modern times, the bow and arrow is still one of the

most formidable weapons in the hands of a skilled man. It has been whispered to me that in the early days of the Desert War, 1940–41, there were those who picked off sentries with the mediaeval weapon.

There is no question that the bow and arrow has still got an edge on a bullet out of an Express rifle; of course it does not shoot as far. It is reputed that the Turks, using short bows with powerful draws, could carry an arrow up to a thousand yards. But, at that distance, there was no accuracy.

At short range, an arrow is incomparably more effective than any bullet. A high velocity bullet fired into water at a fish will be diverted by gravity. An arrow, correctly placed, will go centre straight on target through about six feet of water. The Americans, who have experimented far more carefully than we have, have shown that a well-directed hunting-headed arrow is the most certain way of bringing down game, even big game. An American archer Howard Hill, hunting on foot, dropped an elephant dead in its tracks with an arrow through the heart at forty yards. The quarry may travel but, at the end, it always falls. The penetration of the arrowhead is fatal.

None of the ancient yew bows, the dominant weapons in a succession of battles in the middle ages, survives. They were counted the weapon of the serf. The peasants had to be forced to exercise their skill for purpose of war. When powder and shot was thought to be more effective the yew bows were used to fuel the cottage fires.

The Establishment, as usual, were blind. They were grateful that a poacher's skill should be forgotten. They were glad that powder and shot, available only to the few, should be confined to themselves. As a consequence, we lost a tradition.

I think that there is no doubt that the best archers in mediaeval times achieved everything that is reputed of them: they could split a hazel wand at four hundred paces, shoot an apple off a son's head, cut the rope round the neck of a man on the gallows. There *were* Robin Hoods.

And Robin Hoods exist now. We call them trick shots. In the film business they are in high demand. Men like Howard Hill, who could consistently split a flying plate with an arrow. Men who can be relied upon, in a Robin Hood adventure, to put an arrow into the cork-lined surcoat of a mounted extra.

I was bitten by only a temporary interest. It happened at much the same time that I remember Jack Hawkins, the actor, telling me that in a part as a heroic figure in a period film set in the Middle East, he had to appear as an archer himself. The expert who was to advise him was delayed. So as not to hold up the making of the film, Jack drew his bow without advice. He did not know that it was necessary to put a leather brace on his forearm, and use a leather tab on his drawing finger. Inevitably the string tore the skin off him. A bow, in the hands of an amateur, can behave as nastily as a game gun in the charge of somebody who has not learnt how to take recoil.

I had the good fortune to be instructed by Frank Bilson, a former champion archer of England. He provided me with a short composite bow, far more advanced than anything the archers used at Crecy, and taught me the elements of the game in the gardens of the Royal Toxophilite Society in London.

Time has changed the art. The English long bow, so called because it was as long as the man using it, loses strength with use. Today, a self-bow (a bow made of a single limb of wood like yew or, more likely, degame), is an excellent sort of bow to start with. But if you become a serious archer, entering for target shooting on competition ranges, the obvious choice is a steel or composite bow. They shoot, like the modern rifle, with a greater regularity of performance. Modern arrows of light alloy tubing are much more consistent in weight and performance than wooden shafts.

I fancy that the old archers shot by instinct. We know that they pulled their long bows from the ear. Today, the archer pulls back the bowstring to the centre of his chin. The aim is with the right eye, which is about five inches above the line of the arrow. The game is to make aiming marks on the bow about five inches above the handle (which is roughly the same distance between eye and chin). It is good for up to twenty yards, but you have to modify it for longer distances, making allowances for windage and the idiosyncrasies of every individual shaft. In fact, this is exactly the same principle as the rifle shots employ at Bisley, except that the margin of error is rather greater.

The fletching of every arrow has slight variations. It is necessary in target shooting to number every one in your quiver, and to know its individual ways. The target arrows used today all look level enough. They are not. The champions know each as they would one of their own children. They know the mood of their bows in differing conditions. A pull of thirty pounds will do for a novice. Stronger men will draw up to seventy-five pounds. It is a great sport.

At first you will almost fold up with the effort of drawing a bow. You catch yourself trembling with the effort. You can rap your fingers bracing the string into the nocks. You can get into a mess just drawing an arrow from the quiver over your shoulder. Until you get into the rhythm of it, loosing off six arrows is a physical effort. A target archer shoots 144 arrows (six dozen at 100 yards, four dozen at 80 yards and two dozen at 60 yards).

There is no doubt that this is one of the healthiest sports a man can enjoy. A bow with a light draw is an ideal exercise for women as well. Good Queen Bess hunted deer with it. And I cannot imagine a better sport for someone with chest trouble, unless it be the cowboy game of spinning ropes. But archery is basic English.

I never took my bow to game. I did not practise enough. I never had any interest in the crossbow which, with its winding mechanism, is essentially a weakling's weapon. But archery is a sport, a heritage of our history, and one which is more rewarding than most. If you can come good at it, a bow is a wonderful weapon. Frank Bilson goes rabbiting with his.

23

MY LIFELONG LOVE AFFAIR WITH THE HIGHLANDS

My love of lonely places – the country where everybody knows what everybody else is up to – public knowledge about the killing of a stag, a sheep and a salmon – the Forth Road Bridge brings us closer – August at King's Cross – where the sky cries but nobody comes home wet – friendly adders – the tartan lunatics.

The telephone book of the Highlands of Scotland is not much thicker than a cigarette packet. Yet of all the places in the world that I have travelled, my heart belongs there, somewhere north of Perth.

Admittedly I have a taste for isolation. As a journalist I have always been conscious that I have failed, more or less, when I have been assigned to report on the crowded conurbations of society from London to New York, from Paris to Bombay, from Rome to Teheran, or the once supposedly romantic Orient Express across Europe to Istanbul. I am not made of the stuff that makes gossip columnists. I have discovered that I pull out the best in myself, such as it is, in lonely places.

Looking back, I have richer memories of the Great Slave Lake in the North-West Territories of Canada, of the Kalahari in the unsurveyed areas of Africa, of the jungle lands of India, of the Jordanian desert, than I ever had of the night clubs of 42nd Street in New York, the vulgarities of St Pauli in Hamburg, Berlin in its desperate decadence between the two world wars, or the doubtful sexual pleasures of the Middle East.

Most of my life I have belonged to the chalklands of England, places which have their own rare excellence of quiet. I cannot really tell why, on a train or a car travelling north of the Highland line, I have always felt that I am going home. It may have something to do with genetic traits from Highland ancestors, but I doubt it. The tartan world of the warring clans has only made me laugh. I do not eat my porridge standing up. Some of my best friends have been Campbells. The bagpipes, except from a long, long way away, offend my ear.

The glory that overwhelms me is the beauty of the Highland scene, that wild temperamental country in which from day to day, from hour to hour, the colours of the hills switch out of mist into sunshine and back again. I have driven in Invernesshire when the hills were thick in snow, when the lochs were frozen solid and icicles like giants' fingers hung off every rock; when the sky above was virgin blue. The sun was as warm as a kiss. There is a majesty of nature there that I have found nowhere else on earth.

It is such a grand country and yet, in human terms, such a miniature one. The greatest clan wars of the Highlands involved, at most, a few hundred people. And all the better for that. It remains a parochial world, so parochial that you can scarcely blow your nose without everybody knowing about it. On the train from London to Perth you are just another anonymous traveller. In the breakfast car from Perth to Inverness, if it happens that you are not known, you soon will be. This has often made me grateful that I don't live there; there are times when I prefer to be self-effacing. You haven't a hope of losing yourself in the apparent wilderness of the Highland mountains. Even a golden eagle cannot ascend the sky without being marked.

My son, who shares my affection for those wayward mistresses – Invernesshire, Sutherland and Caithness – took it into his head one autumn dawn to climb a mountain in search of a stag. He was in the lodge at Tongue, which is as far north as you can get on the mainland, until you reach the Pole. Halfway up a mountain, its name I forget, he got a seven-pointer in the sights of his rifle. He had never killed a stag before. Alone he gralloched it and carted it on his shoulders back to the lodge in time for breakfast.

The significance of this story in the Highland landscape is that I was briefly his guest when it happened. The following morning I drove south. I stopped at various remote houses for a drachm. In every single one they had already heard the story of how Max, single-handed, had bagged the stag. They also knew, and at that time I didn't, that a friend of mine who had taken a forest on the other side of Scotland had been taken ill. I can only suppose that the grouse, who travel enormous distances in the shooting season, had put them in the picture.

This sort of thing has happened to me again and again. On the breakfast car travelling north, when I had just completed a novel entitled *Cork on the Water*, in which I believed that I had safely disguised the area I was writing about, I was told that 'we all know that *your* river, which you call the Edendale in the book, is a marriage of the Helmsdale and the Naver'. Worse, they identified old so-and-so there, who were characters in the book.

For me, the personal way in which the Highlands work was never illustrated better than on an occasion in which I was the guest of a laird, who owned a long stretch of the Afric (before the dam was built). When we arrived at Inverness, he immediately went down to the netsmen at the mouth to the sea, and paid them to take off their nets for twenty-four hours. It was about twenty miles to the lodge on the river bank. But, when we arrived, Maclennan the keeper was waiting to welcome us. 'They're here, sir,' he greeted us. The fish had run upstream faster than we could drive there.

Incidentally, it was the same stream where I was once accompanied by a Cockney photographer. I instructed him not to open his mouth, in a rather superior house party, without consulting me under his breath. As we walked along the bank towards the lodge, a salmon showed. Bert exploded, 'Christ, Mac, look at that bloody cod.'

I thought that it was a secret that during the war, I had shot, with a deerstalking rifle, a sheep which was a rogue from the flock. The farmer had given me permission, in those food-rationing days, to remove it. Let's be fair. I shot the wild animal at two hundred yards. When I brought it home for skinning and butchering, two doctors in our party – surgeons too – had apologised for putting their penknives through its heart. Everybody soon knew.

One day I went fishing on a Highland stream with a beautiful young woman who could not have cared less about what was going on. She read a book while I flogged the water. When at last I got into a fish, I persuaded her to put down her book and to take my rod. It was a memorable fight, in which I went nearly haywire begging her to hold up the rod point, to keep below him, to let the line run, not to think she had got him as soon as she saw him. At last, wading up to my thighs, I gaffed the fish. When I landed it, she burst into tears and kissed it. She was a fisherman ever after. And I have reason to believe that *that* story, too, is still told in Highland fishing huts.

I have a mind to tell you how I risked my neck climbing the piers of the Forth Road Bridge while it was still being built. It was on its way to bringing the Highlands, for better or for worse, a little closer to the rest of us down south.

August is reckoned to be the height of the Highland season. It is the month when, in the early morning, on the platform of King's Cross station in London, the smell of the pine needles in 'capers', the smell of heather in grouse, and the wet smell of Labrador retrievers brought down south fill the arid air of the metropolis. I never liked it, that world of open places confined to boxes and leads. The dogs out of the trains look unhappy. The grouse and the capers smell the way they do because they have been taken out of their natural environment. 'The Glorious Twelfth', so called, is a little thing.

It is not the date to shoot grouse when the young birds are not wise enough to defeat the guns. September is the month to try your hand at the most difficult bird which flies. I have often thought, with a gun in my hand, that it is a pleasure to miss him. It is fair-do's when you can catch him, with the wind in his tail, travelling perhaps sixty miles an hour just over the tops of the heather.

I have never regretted shooting grouse in difficult conditions. Grouse flourish where the old heather is burnt, and the old birds are killed to make way for a new generation. Grouse were thin on the ground on the moors until good keeping made life easier for them. It is, alas, sad that the Forestry Commission, rather than shooting them are now making life difficult for them. On the moors the growth of the conifers drives them out.

While, theoretically, autumn in the Highlands is the best season of the year, I don't go with the theory. On the east coast the climate is surprisingly gentle, even though it is cold. True, in the winter of 1977, the area had hard weather, which it completely escaped during the great frost in England in 1962–63. The west is usually full of rain. But what does it matter?

In the hills, where the sky so often cries, I have no recollection of ever coming home wet. Damp, yes. It is a damp in sympathy with the peat bogs, the heather and the bog cotton. In front of the lodge fire, tweeds steam like the warm wool of the upland sheep. But all is clean, fantastically clean, in that soft climate.

I have cursed it in high summer when the clegs and the flies haunting the woodlands and the bracken have driven me off the river. I remember a time when I cut my line on a good salmon rather than face the black fly any longer. At its worst, when the sun is high, the insects can make a crystal stream quite intolerable. At its best, when the turbulent white waters rise high and the wind blows cold, you can feel twice the man you are.

It is a place in which I have always felt at peace. In truth, I have invaded it to shoot grouse and kill salmon. But, deep down inside me, I was not there for sport. I was there because *it* was there, that purple country changing with every whiff of the wind, where every rock told a story. I recollect feeling quite happy when I missed an easy chance to make a right–and–left at a pair of capercailzie. It was their country.

In Sutherland I was once sent out with my gun up the hill to look for a wild cat. I found him, with his barred tail, outside his lair. But I did not shoot; I admired the ruffian, the symbol of the county, too much.

In youth, one shoots anything that walks or flies. In age you throw up your gun. I remember shooting adders because, as I told you earlier, one of them bit my dog. I would not do it now.

In the Highlands you are likely to share your luncheon with them all over the moors. Enough that an adder will never bite you except out of fear. If you counted all the people in this country who have been bitten by an adder, you would be hard put to it to find a hundred. The people who have died from adder bite in the past sixty years number seven, six of them children.

I have come to regard snakes as pretty things (they are first cousins to birds) which we ought to cherish. I think of them as I think of Fly Agaric (*Amanita muscaria*), that poisonous fungus, the stool of the pixies which ornaments so many of the birch woods of the Highlands. The red and white spotted cap is one of the most glorious things in nature.

I have never had quite the same sympathy with the 'Nats' – I could spell it another way – who want to put a Scottish Nationalist Party into power. The absurdity of the movement is that our peoples have been intermarried so long, it is almost impossible to decide what constitutes an Englishman or a Scot. It can only be an attitude of mind. North of the border it certainly exists.

I remember listening to two formidable ladies at a party in Inverness making every insulting comment that they could think of about the Highlanders. At last I ventured to enquire whether they were not Highlanders themselves. They replied, 'We are Vikings.' Eric Linklater, that distinguished Scottish author, capped it for me. 'We Orcadians,' he said, 'put stomach into the Highlanders.' So there you have it. They cannot even agree amongst themselves.

In my English, only vaguely Scottish way, I used to watch old Lochiel, chief of the Cameron clan, haunting the tartan shop outside the Station Hotel in Inverness. He accosted every tourist he saw buying a car rug in the Cameron tartan to enquire whether he was entitled to carry it. The old boy himself was dominated by the tartan tradition. It was a family thing that he and his wife, Lady Hermione, had to be piped to bed. Their bagpiper, himself of advanced years, did the job earlier and earlier. In the end, Lochiel and his wife followed him into the bedroom, waiting to creep out again when the piper had gone to his early rest.

The clan world, a mad mad world, remains an enchanting one. There was one Cameron who named all his eleven sons Donald, to make sure that his name survived him. At Blair Atholl, they once seeded the hills by firing acorns and the rest out of cannons. I have fond memories of the House of Tongue, where every room was lined with the green tartan of the Sutherlands.

I suppose it is true that people take on the colour of the scenery about them. So many of them are larger than life. So much of the scenery is too good to be true.

24

SOUVENIRS

My Game Book – how I lost interest in it – game counters – the passing of the craftsman-made rods and reels – the charm of saving old things – angler's gadgets – fishing tackle for antique collectors – G. E. M. Skues and his taste in trout rods.

On my twenty-first birthday, I was presented with a fat leather-bound volume. It had my name on it embossed in gold, and was binding hundreds of thick cream pages, ruled out and squared. The volume would enable me to keep a lifetime record of fur, fin and feather which fell to my gun and rod. It was to be my Game Book, and a formidable prospect of vast and varied bags it offered. For a time, not without adolescent embarrassment, I kept the record, perforce passing over the columns, listing pheasant, partridge, grouse, salmon, sea trout and red deer, and giving myself a solitary mention under 'Various' with an entry such as a grey squirrel. On 'big days' my bag might be three rabbits and a jack snipe. Once, shooting in the corn stubble, I had eighteen wood-pigeons and one pheasant which, for respectability, I postponed in the record to October 1. There was an occasional mallard, and a tufted duck, which I was so pleased with that I glued one of the feathers into the space provided. Still, the record of my sporting achievements was pitifully bare. Even stretching my fisherman's ruler, I could not measure a trout above eight inches.

As time went on, I recorded the entries in an increasingly desultory manner. When I could have recorded sizeable bags of grouse and pheasant, salmon and sea trout, red deer and even more exotic beasts, I had lost interest. My Game Book survives now with only a few of its pages marked with my paltry little triumphs. As a record, it didn't seem to matter.

On greater estates the Game Books are, of course, important. They determine the value of the sporting rights. Looking back, I could wish now that I had kept a close record of the trout and salmon, especially the salmon, which have fallen to my rod, with details of the beat, the state of the water, weather, temperature, and the size of lure with which they were killed. That is information of value to all fishermen. But in game shooting, only the total bag matters. Individual performance, much of it wishful thinking, is at best self-gratification.

True, there was a time when I kept a game counter in my pocket. I had a pretty silver one, made in Victorian times, with little clocks to mark up the kill of pheasants and partridges, rabbits and hares. It had a certain value, after a big drive, to help the pick-up at the stand. But I haven't used it for years. It is just one of the souvenirs which have collected in my gunroom cupboards and fishing boxes, mementoes of adventures which evoke more memories for me than a Game Book, however carefully kept, could ever do.

Although I do not think that I am a mean man, although most of the gear I have stored away in tackle boxes and gun drawers is admittedly stuff I am unlikely to use again, I loathe parting with any of it, even to my son and heir who shares my disposition for sporting pursuits. I have squirrelled away old brass cartridge cases, pigeon decoys, ferret lines and collars, gun-cleaning gear, rabbit snares, cartridge belts, old gunbags and game bags, and even targets I used for practice. And in common with most anglers, I have acquired enough tackle to last half-a-dozen anglers' lifetimes.

If I had been told, when I was given my Game Book, that I would fish into a generation in which split cane rods, Hardy's Perfect reels and even gut casts were to become collectors' pieces, I would have thought it as improbable as the passing of the Rolls Royce (although that nearly happened too). I have never accustomed myself to fish with nylon as happily as with silkworm gut, which was so much stiffer. The new floating lines are undoubtedly superior, as they are also much more expensive than the old Kingfisher's and the like, which went tacky after a season or two. I have never used a fibreglass rod, nor am I likely to as my old split canes will last me out.

I still have a Grant's Vibration salmon rod, a greenheart with no joints which splices together with wire or, better still, with camera tape, and is I think the loveliest, softest rod, especially in heavy water, that an angler can use. Alas, they are not made any more. I got mine secondhand when the first fibreglass rods were introduced. In the early days of television, I remember that A. G. Street demonstrated one of them playing a girl pulling against him in a swimming pool. The rod bust as soon as he gave her the butt. We thought that glass rods would be no good. Now they are used by every international fly-casting champion.

I still treasure anglers' gadgets, as I do a little box with magnetic points to hold the hooks which I got from the famous shop Abercrombie and Fitch in New York (now, like Hardy's of Alnwick, no more). I still use a pigskin fly book which belonged a hundred years ago to an Ulster medical man. And I have a lovely leather wallet, with the patina of age, described as *The Companion to Alfred Ronald's Fly Fisher's Entomology*. It was published in the middle of the nineteenth century. It names the appropriate trout flies for each month of the season, with enchanting names like the Peacock Fly, Cow Dung Fly, Spider Fly, Hawthorn Fly, Turkey Brown, as well as some of the still familiar names today. Opposite each description is a parchment pocket, containing six specimens of the artificials tied on gut.

I am not aware whether fishing tackle has yet attracted the same attention from antique collectors as old firearms have. But the craze, as it has for other survivals of the past, must come soon. Moral: look after old fishing tackle if you have any. Never again will there be those craftsmen who made the fly and spinning reels of Hardy, Farlow and Ogden Smith. And if you have a Leonard split cane trout rod, you have what the great Itchen fisherman, G. E. M. Skues, described as the best rod ever made. I have fished with one, and I agree with him that I have never handled a rod which bent more sweetly or threw a more rhythmic curve of silk line in the air. They were fabricated in New York State by a craftsman who was said to have emigrated to the United States from Hardy's. Skues used one of his rods but, eclectic as he was, he wasn't content with the American rings and fittings. He had the canes remounted by Hardy's in Northumberland.

I am glad I didn't keep up my Game Book. Without benefit of a record, I have more enjoyed remembering what I have remembered here.